The Kuyper Center Review

New Essays in Reformed Theology and Public Life

The Kuyper Center Review publishes substantial essays of a historical or critical kind that relate the tradition of Reformed theology to issues of public life. Although it will take a special interest in the writings of Abraham Kuyper (1837-1920) and in the neo-Calvinist style of thought that he initiated, the aim is also to provide a vehicle for the widest-ranging exploration of the history and contemporary relevance of Reformed theology to important topics in politics, economics, and culture. Contributions from a variety of disciplines — history, philosophy, the humanities, and social sciences, as well as theology — are warmly welcomed.

The Kuyper Center Review

VOLUME 5 *Church and Academy*

Edited by

Gordon Graham

William B. Eerdmans Publishing Company
Grand Rapids, Michigan / Cambridge, U.K.

Published 2015 by
Wm. B. Eerdmans Publishing Co.
2140 Oak Industrial Drive N.E., Grand Rapids, Michigan 49505 /
P.O. Box 163, Cambridge CB3 9PU U.K.

Printed in the United States of America

21 20 19 18 17 16 15 7 6 5 4 3 2 1

Library of Congress Cataloging-in-Publication Data

Church and academy / edited by Gordon Graham.
pages cm. — (The Kuyper Center review; volume 5)
Includes bibliographical references.
ISBN 978-0-8028-7245-6 (pbk.: alk. paper)
1. Education (Christian theology) — Congresses.
2. Kuyper, Abraham, 1837-1920. — Congresses.
3. Bavinck, Herman, 1854-1921 — Congresses.
4. Bonhoeffer, Dietrich, 1906-1945 — Congresses.
I. Graham, Gordon, 1949 July 15 — editor.

BT738.17.C48 2015
261.5 — dc23

2014044386

www.eerdmans.com

Contents

Editorial vii

Contributors xi

Dread, Hope, and the African Dream: An Ecumenical Collage 1
H. Russel Botman

F. W. J. Schelling: A Philosophical Influence on Kuyper's Social Thought 26
Dylan Pahman

The Pulpit, the Lectern, and the Sickbed: Comparing Dietrich Bonhoeffer and Herman Bavinck on Church and Academy 44
Javier A. Garcia

The Heart of the Academy: Herman Bavinck in Debate with Modernity on the Academy, Theology, and the Church 62
Marinus de Jong

Not without the Church as Institute: The Relevance of Abraham Kuyper's Ecclesiology for Christian Public and Theological Responsibilities in the Twenty-first Century 76
Ad de Bruijne

Evolution as a Bone of Contention between Church and Academy: How Abraham Kuyper Can Help Us Bridge the Gap 92
Gijsbert van den Brink

A Queen without a Throne? Harnack, Schlatter, and Kuyper on Theology in the University 104
Michael Bräutigam

Kuyper on the Teaching of History 119
Harry Van Dyke

Abraham Kuyper and the Idea of a Christian Scholar 130
Gordon Graham

Editorial

"Church and Academy" was the Abraham Kuyper Center for Public Theology conference theme in 2013. There are few themes more directly related to Kuyper's calling, his ambition, and his remarkable achievements. Indeed, it might be argued that it is in the sphere of the academy that we find his most enduring accomplishment. Though his greatest claims to fame are undoubtedly those of an inspirational church leader, a politician of genius, and an indefatigable journalist, the many things he accomplished in these arenas were context relative, and were for the most part absorbed as the years passed. The Doleantie, for example, that he so spectacularly led out of the Dutch Reformed Church was eventually subsumed within a larger grouping, a grouping that 120 years later included the very church from which it separated. Thanks to Kuyper's organizational skills, his newly founded Anti-Revolutionary Party was far ahead of its time. For that very reason, of course, others quickly came to emulate it, so that the period of political power to which it led was relatively brief, and the party itself no longer exists. The two newspapers that Kuyper edited so effectively for so many decades have ceased to publish, and we now live in a world of social media in which the skills of traditional journalism are increasingly redundant.

In sharp contrast, the VU University in Amsterdam that Kuyper created has not merely survived; it has grown to take its place alongside some of the best-known universities in the world, and anyone visiting it today will find a bust of Kuyper in the main stairwell. To list the academy ahead of Kuyper's other achievements for this reason, however, is somewhat misleading. The modern VU is not only geographically a considerable distance from its original location; it is housed in buildings vastly different in size and style, and hence in "feel," from those that formed its original home. More importantly, the academic program that its scientists, scholars, teachers, and students now follow retains relatively little — almost nothing, some would say — of the original vision that Kuyper had for it. In reality, it would be difficult to say that VU differs in any very striking way from a long list of modern European universities with decidedly contrasting histories. While there is no doubt that Kuyper made a significant contribution to the life of the academy in his own day, that day is past, and it is far from evident that the foundation he laid for the institution he created continues to influence the life of the academy in the present.

Two key changes between then and now stand out and give rise to two related issues. The Netherlands can no longer be plausibly described as a Christian country. The degree to which it has become secularized, consequently, makes the maintenance of an avowedly and distinctively Christian university almost impossible. One effect of this is that the role of theology within the university cannot be what Kuyper thought it could and must be. The deep cultural change is demonstrable, and the insecurity of theology as a subject in the modern academy scarcely any less contestable. Yet we can still intelligibly ask this question: Do these changes mean that Kuyper's vision, and the thinking that underlay it, have nothing to say to a world so greatly altered from the one for which he framed them? In one way or another, all the papers in this fifth volume of the *Kuyper Center Review* relate to this question.

The opening paper is the text of the lecture given by Professor Russel Botman, winner of the Abraham Kuyper Prize in 2013. The prize is not reserved for distinguished Kuyperian scholars. It is awarded to individuals whose faith has led them to excel in one of the sovereign "spheres" around which Kuyper thought a free and stable society must be built. Botman, accordingly, does not draw directly on Kuyper or the experience of the Netherlands. Yet common ground is not far to seek. He writes as both an academic leader and a professional theologian shaped by the Dutch Reformed tradition. His reflections arise from a context in which Kuyper was steeped, and at the same time show themselves to be relevant to one of the most important changes in the political contours of the modern world — the abolition of apartheid and the transformation of South Africa. Obliquely, then, Botman's paper is testimony to the continuing relevance of the kind of theological formation that Kuyper strove to secure.

The other papers tackle the issue of the continuing academic relevance of Kuyper's Christian vision and theological orientation more directly. Some seek to deepen our understanding of that vision and orientation by placing it in its historical milieu, while at the same time putting it in a broader intellectual and theological context, finding connections and drawing comparisons with other notable theological thinkers. Some address specific debates that both raged in Kuyper's time and continue to do so in ours. Others consider more abstractly the merits and demerits of the ideas that he advanced and their applicability to contemporary circumstances.

Taken together, the papers show beyond doubt that Kuyper, his contemporaries, and his times are of deep and enduring historical interest. But they also draw attention to the fact that many of the issues with which he was concerned are issues that remain to be resolved. The Church's relationship to and its role in the academy are topics of continuing intellectual and social significance. Indeed, it might be said without exaggeration that these are topics of pressing importance for both sides of the relationship. The Church needs to understand the proper place of education and scholarship in its life, work, and witness. But the academy too must be able to give a cogent account of its meaning and purpose for the lives of those who populate the societies that support it. On these issues, the papers further serve to show, there is still a lot to be learned from what Kuyper and his contemporaries had to say about them.

In Memoriam: Hayman Russel Botman

Russel Botman was Rector and Vice-Chancellor of Stellenbosch University, one of South Africa's leading higher-education institutions. He was appointed Rector in 2007 and reappointed for a second term in 2012. His sudden and unexpected death on 28 June 2014 was a very great loss to both church and academy in South Africa, and the wider world.

Born in Bloemfontein in 1953, Botman received his secondary education in Kliptown, Soweto. He studied at the University of the Western Cape, where he served as a member of the Students' Representative Council in 1976, the year of youth uprisings against apartheid. He graduated with a Ph.D. in Theology, and rose to become Dean of the Faculty of Religion and Theology. In 2000, he was appointed Professor in Missiology, Ecumenism, and Public Theology at Stellenbosch University, serving as Vice-Rector for Teaching from 2002 until his appointment as Rector in 2007. As Rector he was an enthusiastic and effective proponent of the idea that science should drive Africa's development, and prime mover behind Stellenbosch University's HOPE Project, a science-for-society initiative.

An ordained minister of the Uniting Reformed Church in Southern Africa, Russel Botman was President of the South African Council of Churches from 2003 to 2007, served as Research Consultant to the World Alliance of Reformed Churches, and was the founding Director of the Beyers Naudé Centre for Public Theology. He published widely on human rights, reconciliation, human dignity, the Belhar Confession, and social justice.

In 2013 Professor Botman visited the United States to receive an honorary degree from Hope College, in Holland, Michigan, and Princeton Theological Seminary's Abraham Kuyper Prize for Excellence in Theology and Public Life. The lecture he gave on that occasion is published for the first time in this issue of the *Kuyper Center Review.*

Gordon Graham
Princeton Theological Seminary

Contributors

H. Russel Botman was Rector and Vice-Chancellor of Stellenbosch University, South Africa, until his sudden death in 2014. He gained a Ph.D. in Theology from the University of the Western Cape and was an ordained minister of the Uniting Reformed Church.

Michael Bräutigam, Ph.D., is teaching assistant at the University of Edinburgh. His doctoral work examines the Christology of Adolf Schlatter. An ordained minister of the Free Church of Scotland, he is particularly interested in Kuyper's contribution of a public theology for the church today. He was the 2011 and 2012 visiting Puchinger scholar at Princeton Theological Seminary.

Gijsbert van den Brink is Professor for the Theology of Reformed Protestantism at the Protestant Theological University in Amsterdam, and Associate Professor of Christian Doctrine at the Faculty of Theology, VU University Amsterdam. Along with his colleague Cornelis van der Kooi, he authored an introduction to Christian dogmatics (*Christelijke dogmatiek,* Zoetermeer, 2012), an English translation of which is in preparation with Eerdmans.

Ad (A. L. Th.) de Bruijne is professor at the Theological University Kampen. He studied philosophy and theology in Utrecht and Kampen, and from 1986 until 1997 he served two congregations in the Netherlands as a minister. He took his Ph.D. from Leiden University (2006) with a study on the theme of Christendom in the political theology of Oliver O'Donovan. His main field of research is public theology.

Javier A. Garcia is a doctoral student in Christian theology at the University of Cambridge, researching the confluence of Reformed and Lutheran elements in Dietrich Bonhoeffer's ecclesiology. He is the author of "A Critique of Mannermaa on Luther and Galatians" (*Lutheran Quarterly* 27.1 [2013]).

Gordon Graham is Henry Luce III Professor of Philosophy and the Arts at Princeton Theological Seminary, and Chair of the Advisory Board of the Kuyper Center for Theology and Public Life. His publications include *Universities: The Recovery of an Idea* (Imprint Academic, 2008), and *Wittgenstein and Natural Religion* (Oxford University Press, 2014).

Marinus de Jong obtained his M.A. in systematic theology from the Theologische Universiteit in Kampen, the Netherlands. His research focuses on neo-Calvinism and Pentecostal theology. Previously he studied at Wycliffe Hall, Oxford, and at the Faculté Jean Calvin, Aix-en-Provence.

Dylan Pahman is Assistant Editor of the *Journal of Markets & Morality*, a Research Associate at the Acton Institute, and a Fellow of the Sophia Institute.

Harry Van Dyke (D.Litt., VU University Amsterdam) is Professor of History Emeritus at Redeemer University College, Ancaster, Ontario.

Dread, Hope, and the African Dream: An Ecumenical Collage

H. Russel Botman

Introduction

My theological reflection has always been dominated by questions related to *kairos* moments — what exactly such *kairoi* are and the way they impact on how we express our faith in the midst of the *chronos* of our lives. Paul Tillich describes a *kairos* as a "fulfilled moment, the moment of time approaching us as fate and decision"[1] and "a moment of history . . . pregnant with a new understanding of the meaning of history and life."[2] For Tillich, *kairoi* — right or opportune moments, moments of truth — clearly refer to those moments of crisis in history that create an opportunity for, or even demand, an existential decision.

Although Tillich suggests that a *kairos* "should express the feeling of many people," *kairoi* are also personal, existential moments in the *chronos* of life. Being a theologian, the *kairoi* in my life are usually, as may be expected, ac-

1. Paul Tillich, "Kairos and Logos," in *The Interpretation of History,* trans. N. A. Rasetzki and Elsa L. Talmey (New York and London: Charles Scribner's Sons, 1926), 129.

2. Paul Tillich, *Systematic Theology,* vol. 3 (Chicago: University of Chicago Press, 1963), 369.

This is the text of the Kuyper Prize Lecture, 2013, dedicated to my mentors, Jaap Durand and Dirk Smit, South Africa. Special thanks go to my wife, Beryl, and to my children. Gratitude also goes to Len Hansen, Desmond Thompson, Nico Koopman, and Dirk Smit for adding the final touches to this lecture. — H.R.B.

companied by some sort of theological reflection. As a *Reformed* theologian, being part of a tradition that practices a theology that is deeply personal (never merely private), existential (never disinterested), congregational (never dislocated), ecumenical (never parochial), and contextual (never ahistorical and abstracted),[3] my personal *kairoi* also share these characteristics.

What I want to present to you here is an ecumenical collage of two of my *kairos* moments over the past thirty-five years of being a theologian — one at home in South Africa, and the other, interestingly, having its roots here, in Princeton.

But these *kairoi* concern more than me and my faith: they concern my country and my continent; and indeed, in a roundabout way, they concern you, my gracious hosts, your country and continent — in fact, the world at large and what we all hope for and dream of.

A Fable of the Brothers Grimm: The Relationship between Dread and Hope

Before I expand on the detail of this collage, I want to tell a story, one of the fables of the brothers Grimm, and look at three modern reflections on it — from a philosophical and theological perspective. The story is about a young man who went out to learn how to be afraid.[4] He goes through some of the most horrifying experiences that would frighten the living daylight out of any superhero. However, he remains unimpressed as nothing succeeds in frightening him. Then one night, his wife, who loves him deeply, teaches him the meaning of fear when she pours a bucket of cold water full of squirming little fish over him as he sleeps. This is the experience that finally fills him with a nameless horror and an abysmal fear. "Ah!" he exclaimed, "now I know what it is to fear."

Three thinkers have reflected on the meaning of this fairy tale for their contemporaries: Søren Kierkegaard, Ernst Bloch, and Jürgen Moltmann. The first, Kierkegaard, developed the story philosophically in his famous work, *The Concept of Dread:*

3. Cf. H. Russel Botman, "A Cry for Life in a Global Economic Era," in *Reformed Theology: Identity and Ecumenicity,* ed. Wallace M. Alston and Michael Welker (Grand Rapids: Eerdmans, 2003), 375.

4. "The Story of the Youth Who Went Forth to Learn What Fear Was," in *The Complete Grimm's Fairy Tales* (London: Routledge, 1975), 29-39.

> One of Grimm's fairy tales is a story about a lad who went out to seek adventure in order to learn how to shiver with fear. We will let the adventurer go his way without concerning ourselves further about whether he met horror as he went or not. What I should like to say here is that this is an adventure which everyone has to face: the adventure of learning to know how to be afraid, so as not to be lost, either through not having learnt how to fear, or through being completely engulfed by fear. The person who has learnt how to be afraid in the right way has learnt the most important thing of all.[5]

Ernst Bloch reads the fairy tale differently:

> Once upon a time a man went out in order to learn how to be afraid. That was easier to do in times past, when fear was always close at hand. The art of being afraid was something people were terribly proficient in. But now, except where there is a real reason for fear, a more appropriate feeling is expected of us.
>
> The important thing is to learn how to hope. The labor of hope never gives anything up. . . . Hope is higher than fear. It is not passive like fear. Even less is it locked away into pure Nothingness. The emotion of hope goes out of itself. It expands men and women instead of constricting them and hedging them in.[6]

In 1994, a third scholar, theologian Jürgen Moltmann, interpreted the story as the majority of South Africans were making their way toward voting stations for the first time:

> Without fear we should be blind, ruthless and rash. . . . How could we hope for life, liberty and happiness and snatch hopefully at the chances of these things which the future offers, if we did not simultaneously fear death, oppression and misfortune. . . . In this respect the "concept of dread" and "the principle of hope" are not opposites at all.[7]

These three interpretations, by three very different people in very different times, say much about fear and the relationship between fear and hope. Kierkegaard tells us that learning to be afraid is invaluable and absolutely necessary

5. In J. Moltmann, *Experiences of God*, trans. Margaret Kohl (Minneapolis: Augsburg Fortress, 1980), 39.

6. E. Bloch, *The Principle of Hope*, trans. Neville Plaice, Stephen Plaice, and Paul Knight (Oxford: Basil Blackwell, 1986), 1.

7. J. Moltmann, *Jesus Christ for Today's World*, trans. Margaret Kohl (Minneapolis: Fortress, 1994), 52-53.

for living a sustainable life. Bloch contrasts fear with hope, emphasizing the differences between the two and the importance of hope beyond fear. Moltmann bridges the gap between fear and hope, arguing that "dread" and "hope" are not opposites at all, but that it is out of dread, out of fear, that hope is born.

Kairoi as Moments of Fear

More often than not, *kairoi* are moments of fear. According to Albert Nolan, a South African stalwart of the church struggle against apartheid, a *kairos* "is a time of judgment. . . . A time for real fear and trembling. . . . A time of tears and sadness."[8]

In my life I have also experienced *kairoi* such as this. As a young black person in South Africa in the turbulent late-1970s, I studied for the ministry at a university and for a church whose membership was defined along oppressive racial lines. It was 1978, two years after the terrible tragedy when young people took to the streets of Soweto in a desperate attempt to change their future and paid for it with their lives. I participated in a theological seminar where the professor focused our attention on the search for the theological center of apartheid. Having done in-depth reflection on biblical witness and having focused especially on Karl Barth's understanding of reconciliation, the seminar emerged after several days with the dictum that "apartheid is essentially anti-evangelical in that it takes its point of departure in the irreconcilability of people."[9] In the words of fellow-South African theologian Dirk Smit,

> [a]partheid was about separateness, about dividing people, keeping them apart, through legal, social, economic and political measures, thereby denying and destroying any form of unity between them, attempting to resist any form of belonging, solidarity, sharing, mutuality and caring. Apartheid therefore led to separation, to estrangement, to alienation, to a deep lack of mutual understanding and acceptance, resulting in mistrust and suspicion, fear and hurt, even bitterness and hatred, in short, an urgent need for reconciliation, for acceptance and forgiveness, for building bridges over the deep divides separating people.[10]

8. Albert Nolan, *Hope in an Age of Despair* (Maryknoll, NY: Orbis, 2009), 86.

9. Cf. J. W. De Gruchy and C. Villa-Vicencio, *Apartheid Is a Heresy* (Cape Town: David Phillip, 1983), 161-65.

10. D. J. Smit, "What Does It Mean to Live in South Africa and to Be Reformed?" *Reformed World* 58 (2008): 263-83.

Since the nineteenth century, and for most of the twentieth century, my country saw the gradual development and eventual full-scale biblical justification of the church policy and later the public and political policy of apartheid. At the time, much of this was done by the Dutch Reformed Church (DRC) (the *Nederduits Gereformeerde Kerk* [NGK]) in South Africa through a deliberate distortion of the theological tradition of Abraham Kuyper. For us students, this was unacceptable; it was in direct opposition to our faith and our understanding of Scripture. We dreaded the impact it had or may have had on our faith and those around us. We faced a tough conclusion in the public domain at the time: How could we be black and Reformed in that context?[11]

Upon finishing my studies and entering the ministry in the Wynberg congregation of the Dutch Reformed Mission Church (DRMC) — as a section of what we would later transform into the Uniting Reformed Church of Southern Africa was known then — I realized that the same fear, the same dread, faced many "ordinary" members of my congregation, and also our whole church. My personal fear for my faith, for my own future as a young person, and for the faith of my children, my personal *kairos,* I realized, was shared by my whole church.[12]

Under the leadership of Boesak and others, the Alliance of Black Re-

11. A. Boesak, *Black and Reformed: Apartheid, Liberation, and the Calvinist Tradition* (Maryknoll, NY: Orbis Books, 1984).

12. This theology of irreconcilability had quite a lot to do with conflicting interpretations of Kuyper's theology. In 1998 I was one of several scholars from around the world who spoke at a conference at Princeton on "Religion, Pluralism, and Public Life: Abraham Kuyper's Legacy for the 21st Century." In my contribution, "Is Blood Thicker than Justice?," I argued that Abraham Kuyper has had both an oppressive and a liberative influence on South Africa as both main traditions of the South African Reformed Church — Dutch and Reformed as well as Black and Reformed — laid claim to the legacy of Kuyper. The Dutch Reformed Church (DRC), by taking Kuyper's creation theology in combination with the biblical metaphor of the tower of Babel, developed this legacy as a grand natural theological foundation for separateness. I argued that they had, however, not been told that Kuyper had drawn a distinction between the condition of humanity before Babel, on the one hand, and after Christ, on the other. Their mentors did not tell them that Kuyper regarded visible pluriformity as a passing phase in historical development. They had not even been reminded of Kuyper's conviction that unity would triumph as the eventual purpose of God's plan of creation. This was the liberative influence of Kuyper that was uncovered and stressed by a group of South Africans who, in 1981, organized the Alliance of Black Reformed Christians in South Africa (ABRECSA). The Alliance grounded its charter in Kuyper's legacy, and specifically in his concern for social justice. Later, the Confession of Belhar would also strongly emphasize the biblical teaching of social justice and, thus, Kuyper's legacy became part and parcel of the basic tenets of the Confession of Belhar.

formed Christians in South Africa (ABRECSA) was formed in 1981. In this organization we started to embrace Abraham Kuyper's fundamental position expressed in his speech to the Christian Social Congress of 1891:

> When rich and poor stand opposed to each other, Jesus never takes his place with the wealthier, but always stands with the poorer. He is born in a stable; and while foxes have holes and birds have nests, the Son of Man has nowhere to lay his head. . . . Both Christ and his disciples after him (just as the prophets before him) invariably took sides against those who were powerful and living in luxury and for the suffering and oppressed.

In 1982, the draft Confession of Belhar was adopted by the Dutch Reformed Mission Church (DRMC). In its focus on the question of justice and poverty it shifted the attention to Karl Barth's stance, which differed from that of Kuyper in that he argued that God's position was not defined as a partisan siding for the poor against the rich, but as a revelation in the context of injustice and enmity. Therefore, the Confession of Belhar[13] states that in such a context, God reveals God's self as the God of the poor and the downtrodden, the stranger, the orphan and the widow.

Almost ten years after this first *kairos,* I experienced a second *kairos,* one that was also personal, but one I realized I also shared with many others. In 1997, during my first week as a resident scholar here at the Center of Theological Inquiry in Princeton, I walked into the library. I wanted to study the relationship between and dynamics and tensions implied in one's membership of a religious community on the one hand, and one's citizenship of a new democracy on the other.

The first month of my exposure to that library and my discussions with people across different disciplines led to a radical revisioning of my theological paradigm, and this was the beginning of another *kairos* for me. A review of my own life helped me to see how my theological studies, and my personal library, were engulfed by a Reformed theology defined by issues of church-state relationships. Through my intellectual exposure here in Princeton, I came face to face with a new kind of dread: these issues had in fact become almost irrelevant in many theological circles, as we and our faith now had to contend with a much more powerful and sometimes much more subtle adversary, globalization — and more specifically, a certain globalization that has exclusionary potential.

13. Online at http://www.pcusa.org/media/uploads/theologyandworship/pdfs/belhar.pdf.

I began to realize that globalization is a socially constructed economic process that has integrated certain markets (excluding the labor market) and that is dominated by the financial market.[14] It is strengthened and proliferated by the growing interdependence of economics and technology and allows for fast and free movement of capital and valuable information. The forces of globalization have assumed the status of economic necessity; they project an ideological imperative. Globalization as an ideal allows for no alternative measure of thought; it presents itself as the only view on contemporary society. This view redefines humanity as *Homo economicus,* and it influences behavior towards aggressive competitiveness in which only the richest survive, yet claiming that "the trickle-down effect" will solve the problem of poverty — among the weakest!

Theology's primary concern about globalization is not its economic premise, but the kind of society and values it produces. This can be seen in the behavior it promotes and the fragmentation it causes in the moral foundations of communities. Individualism abounds and competition is celebrated. Solidarity and cooperation are sacrificed. In short, exclusionary globalization results in a worldview driven by the rationale of contemporary economics that does not favor, but in fact threatens, the values of inclusive community. My research convinced me that the forces of global exclusion are as dangerous as the marginalization in the first *kairos* of apartheid. These forces share a common victim-blindness and a culpability for sacrificing their victims to a false faith. This filled me with dread, because it too was a matter of faith.[15]

14. For my views on the essence and dangers of globalization, see H. R. Botman, "The *Oikos* in a Global Economic Era: A South African Comment," in *Sameness and Difference: Problems and Potentials in South African Civil Society,* ed. James R. Cochrane and Bastienne Klein, South African Philosophical Studies 1 (Washington, DC: Council for Research in Values and Philosophy, 2000), 269-79.

15. Another "Kuyperian footnote" might help explain what I mean. In "Is Blood Thicker than Justice?," I commented that Kuyper's world is no longer ours, that "we no longer think in terms of an 'organic society' opposed to a 'mechanical' government, but instead we confront the adversarial power of a technological, global society that has left the nation-state superfluous. We can no longer affirm the concept of the sovereignty of God without an equal emphasis on God's freedom and historical vulnerability. As black Reformed people steeped in Dutch Calvinism," I said, we must remember Kuyper's emphasis on social justice. "In a sermon on Matthew 6:24, for example, he warned that Scripture has identified a greater evil than the golden calf: the power of Mammon. One expects nothing from the golden calf yet sacrifices all one's belongings to it. The golden calf at least inspires giving in people. This makes Mammonization a more dangerous idolatry than the naiveté of worshipping the golden calf. Jesus' claim that one cannot serve God and Mammon," I reiterated, "reveals to us the anti-religious nature of economic injustice. It is not about a mere choice for another god, Kuyper argued; it is a choice against God and a denial of God's providence for all people." The most underdeveloped part

Kairos Moments as Moments of Hope

Quoting Nolan above with reference to the first *kairos* was, however, only half the story and half his view. According to him, a *kairos* is not only a time of judgment, but also one of salvation. It may be a time of tears and sadness, but it also is "[a] time to take a stand," as it is "a time fraught with hope and joyful anticipation."[16]

Kairoi *as Moments of Biblical and Contextual Hope*

To return to our fable at the beginning of this lecture, that of the brothers Grimm and the three interpretations thereof — that without fear no sustainable livelihoods are possible (Kierkegaard); that no matter how intense the fear, hope remains higher than fear (Bloch); and that "the concept of dread [fear]" is also not opposed to "the principle of hope" (Moltmann) — as a theologian I had to ask myself, in the midst of each *kairos,* what is the hope I can live by? What would be a Christian understanding of the almost desperate hope against all hope of the Sowetan youths who, empty-handed, took on the might of the security forces of the apartheid government in 1976?

For this one has to, of course, start with the Bible. In 1 Peter 3:14 the author clearly says: "Do not fear what they fear; do not be frightened." Peter calls on us "always," in the face of fear, to "be prepared to give account of the hope that you have" (1 Pet. 3:15). When people fear, Peter seems to say, you shall engage them *always* in the discourse of hope; you shall get them talking about hope; you shall engage them in actions of hope; you shall help them see the signs of hope. This is your Christian responsibility. Always give an account of the hope that is in you, because that hope is not your possession, it belongs to the world, it is hope for the world.

---

of Kuyper's systematic thinking is his integration of questions of economics with Reformed theology. A re-contextualization of the Reformed worldview and action should accept the challenge of coming to terms with global economic exclusion as a sacrifice to Mammon, with Africa first in line. I am convinced that the Mammonization of the market is an urgent matter for theological reflection. "It is no longer merely a matter of ethics. It has become a matter of faith, a matter of Reformed identity. What is at stake in developing a post-Kuyperian worldview is nurturing a less ethnic and more transnational form of Reformed identity. Making this contribution to the worldwide debate will mean justice, truth, and reconciliation for an abandoned continent called Africa. What we need is justice reformed; justice beyond blood."

16. Nolan, *Hope in an Age of Despair.*

The centrality of hope in the Christian gospel is beyond question. It is the middle element of the triad of Christian life that Paul mentions in 1 Corinthians 13:13 ("Meanwhile these three remain, faith, hope, and love"), a triangle with equal corners that energizes Christianity. It replaces all other loyalties. Biblical scholars tell us that an understanding of the social world of Paul is crucial for the interpretation of his use of the triad. According to David M. Bossman, who sees the triad as a set of social values that establishes the norm for Christian life, these images are profoundly Mediterranean.[17] This means that the triad represents a collective, public understanding of Christianity and not a personal, individualistic one. This also means that Paul is writing not about one's personal love, individual faith, or private hopes. Instead, he is speaking of collective and publicly demonstrated faith, hope, and love. On the three elements of Christian identity, there cannot be any argument between Christians from America, South Africa, Brazil, China, or Palestine. They are all, as Christians, people of the triad; the triad is the international mark of Christianity.

However, Paul also moves away from the structure of equality in the triad: "The greatest of these is love" (1 Cor. 13:13). How did this move happen? The answer can be found only by rereading the first letter to the Corinthians. So, let us eavesdrop on the conversation between a distressed apostle and the people he loved. Paul covers serious communal concerns: the abuse of the feast of love; the marginalization of the poor; scary issues of sex and marriage; legal disputes among community members; conflicts of a holier-than-thou nature. In all these questions he is distressed by the level of division, conflict, and class separation in the congregation. In fact, the full story that we find in 1 Corinthians 1–12 is that of lovelessness, enmity, marginalization, and hatred. It is in this context that Paul states, "The greatest of these is love."

Now, whatever is the greatest must be understood as that which is of the greatest importance to the people given their own social condition. In the context of lovelessness, enmity, and hatred, love is the greatest in the triad.

However, we have been witnesses to this critical choice in ministry and public life at different times in history. At certain times the world needs a Martin Luther or John Calvin who proclaims the greatness of *faith* in the triad. In fact, these men emphasized the idea of "faith alone." At other times we need the prophetic voice of Martin Luther King Jr. calling us to *love* above all other things when he speaks of people living in love in the country of the brave — here he sounds very much like Paul. It shows that we have to make a

17. D. M. Bossman, "Paul's Mediterranean Gospel: Faith, Hope, Love," *Biblical Theology Bulletin* 25 (1995): 71-78.

critical contextual decision about the primacy in the triad of Christian public life. Within the context of what has been said thus far, one may formulate it as such: within a *kairos* of dread we need to shuffle around the triad once more; we now need hope. We need to dream once more, a dream of *hope* that we need to confess and act upon.

Hope in the Kairos *of Apartheid*

The first *kairos* I referred to took place during the time of the declaration of the dreaded States of Emergency in South Africa in 1985 and 1986, which John de Gruchy calls "the catalyst for what turned out to be both the final push in the struggle against apartheid and, alongside that, in the Church Struggle" against apartheid. True to the nature of *kairoi* as expressed by Nolan above, it coincided with the acceptance of and the publication of two uniquely South African documents: the Belhar Confession in 1986 (first drafted in 1982) by the DRMC; and the aptly named Kairos Document in 1985.[18]

According to De Gruchy, "the Kairos Document challenged the failure of other churches to actively engage in the struggle against apartheid. But whereas previously, the NGK *(Nederduits Gereformeerde Kerk)* had regarded itself as the custodian of the true Reformed faith, now it was being accused not just of supporting injustice, but also of having become heretical in the process." The Kairos Document condemned the theological and philosophical arguments for apartheid. Both a "state theology" with a national-security ideology and a "church theology" of cheap reconciliation and social harmony were attacked. It also called on the churches to move from protest to action. It therefore is significant that the fourth chapter of the Kairos Document ("Towards a Prophetic Theology") would pronounce that

> At the very heart of the gospel of Jesus Christ and at the very center of all true prophecy is a message of hope. Nothing could be more relevant and more necessary at this moment of crisis in South Africa than the Christian message of hope.[19]

And the Belhar Confession, in the face of the illegitimate convictions of the irreconcilability of humankind, would become — according to one of

18. Online at http://www.sahistory.org.za.

19. The Kairos Document, in *Radical Christian Writings: A Reader,* ed. A. Bradstoc and C. Rowland (Oxford: Blackwell, 2008), 301.

its compilers, Dirk Smit — "a kairos moment of witness on the unifying and reconciling power of the gospel." Thus Belhar confessed:

> We believe:
> - that God has entrusted the church with the message of reconciliation in and through Jesus Christ; that the church is called to be the salt of the earth and the light of the world, that the church is called blessed because it is a peacemaker, that the church is witness both by word and by deed to the new heaven and the new earth in which righteousness dwells;
> - that God's life-giving Word and Spirit has conquered the powers of sin and death, and therefore also of irreconciliation and hatred, bitterness and enmity, that God's life-giving Word and Spirit will enable the church to live in a new obedience which can open new possibilities of life for society and the world;
> - that the credibility of this message is seriously affected and its beneficial work obstructed when it is proclaimed in a land which professes to be Christian, but in which the enforced separation of people on a racial basis promotes and perpetuates alienation, hatred and enmity;
> - that any teaching which attempts to legitimate such forced separation by appeal to the gospel, and is not prepared to venture on the road of obedience and reconciliation, but rather, out of prejudice, fear, selfishness and unbelief, denies in advance the reconciling power of the gospel, must be considered ideology and false doctrine.
>
> Therefore, we reject any doctrine which, in such a situation sanctions in the name of the gospel or of the will of God the forced separation of people on the grounds of race and color and thereby in advance obstructs and weakens the ministry and experience of reconciliation in Christ.

Reconciliation is indeed the heart of the gospel of Christ. However, through our faith in Christ, reconciliation is expressed as love. And a living reconciliation finds its lasting meaning in hope.

For the rest of my life this personal and communal *kairos* moment, this basic conviction of reconcilability and of being reconciled, would steer my work and theological reflection. This was true of my work during the years of my ministry in the Wynberg congregation, my terms first as Assessor and later National Vice-Moderator of the DRMC from 1990 to 1994, as General Secretary of the Church's Commission for Ecumenical Affairs, in my work and interaction with my students as lecturer, and later professor, in the Department of Religion and Society at the University of the Western Cape from 1994 to 1999, and from 2000 as Professor of Missiology, Ecumenism, and Public Theology in the Faculty of Theology at Stellenbosch University (ironically, where much of the South African "theology of the irreconcilability of humankind" was taught for decades, if not born). It was part of my presidency of the South African Council of Churches from 2003 to 2007, my role as founding director of the Beyers Naudé Institute for Public Theology, and, since 2002, it has remained important in my role first as Vice-Rector for Teaching and now Rector and Vice-Chancellor of Stellenbosch University.

Hope and the Kairos *of Exclusionary Globalization*

The second *kairos* I refer to above, the second moment of dread — that of the impact of exclusionary globalization on our world and on our lives and faith as Christians — also was and remains a moment rich with potential and pregnant with possibilities. These possibilities for hope found expression in two declarations of the then World Alliance of Reformed Churches (WARC), and in my own reflections on and rediscovery of the value of community and the theological themes of the *oikos* and covenant of God.

From 2001 to 2004, as Research Consultant to the WARC, I participated in its Project on Covenanting for Justice in the Economy and the Earth, which led to the acknowledgment of a *kairos* and a *processus confessionis* within that body. But, even before that, the Southern African Alliance of Reformed Churches met in the small mining town of Kitwe in northern Zambia during my term as its moderator (1990-1998). Here the Alliance, quoting directly from the Belhar Confession, appealed to the world community of Reformed believers, congregations, and churches to see the economic injustices in our world and the careless destruction of creation, to discern the challenge for their faith, and to respond by concrete action. Several important implications for the Reformed faith already became clear in Kitwe. Dirk Smit describes the deliberations at Kitwe as follows:

> The three themes that had been at stake in the apartheid struggle now took on new faces and forms — on a global scale. Questions concerning living unity, real reconciliation and compassionate justice were again challenging Reformed believers and churches, but now on a much larger scale. Again, it became important to discern, to confess and to be willing to critique, resist and confront, in the words of Kitwe, to see, to judge and to act, in order to help bring hope to the hopeless. Together with many other voices from all over the world, the voice crying from Kitwe, using language from

Belhar, now lamented a whole continent, indeed suffering humanity and creation itself.[20]

Later, in 1997, at the 23rd Assembly of the WARC in Debrecen, Hungary, the cry voiced at Kitwe would become the voice of the ecumenical Reformed community, asking whether its own faith was not indeed at stake in these challenges. And, returning to Africa in 2004, the Council later adopted the well-known document, "Covenanting for Justice in the Economy and the Earth"[21] at the 24th Accra General Council of the WARC. The body's General Council was very much under the influence of the visit by its delegates to the slave dungeons of Elmina and the Cape Coast, and of the cries of "never again." They therefore made a new "faith commitment."

In their "Letter from Accra,"[22] the official message of the 2004 General Council sent as a pastoral letter to all member churches, they further explained and motivated this commitment. They saw the presence of the Reformed tradition in these castles, and they were deeply challenged by the radical contradictions between the faith and the actions of their Reformed forebears. The Council thus began to discern that similar contradictions may still be present in their own churches, and in their own lives. They became aware of their ecumenical unity, yet at the same time of the deep need for reconciliation amongst them — both with their past and with one another. They painfully realized how "today's world is divided between those who worship in comfortable contentment and those enslaved by the world's economic injustice and ecological destruction who still suffer and die." They acknowledged that "millions of others in our congregations live lives as inattentive to this suffering as those who worshipped God on the floor above slave dungeons." They discerned that this was not just another "issue" to be "addressed"; in this challenge their own faith was at stake, their confession that Jesus Christ is Lord. "That is why we find in the Bible a constant criticism of idolatry, emphasized in our Reformed tradition." They reflected at length on how this would affect the ways in which Reformed churches see their own mission today. "Such a confession also sends us forth with new eyes of faith into the world. Mission, it can be said, is embodied in the life of the church in the world. In Accra it was recognized that living according to what we say we believe changes our understanding of mission today. How can we share the message and liberating love of Christ's

20. Online at http://oikoumene.net.
21. Online at http://warc.jalb.de.
22. Online at http://warc.jalb.de.

life in those places where suffering and death seem to reign?" It became clear that this mission calls them into "new and fuller forms of unity" — "more than ever, faithful mission today requires our connection — really it demands bonds of belonging — between one another as churches."

These experiences and events all spoke loudly and clearly to me, especially in light of my rediscovery of the value of community and the theological themes of the *oikos* of God, covenant, and the kingdom of God. The term "economy" derives from the Greek *oikos-nomos* (the regulation of the *oikos*). Economics *(oikonomia)* is essentially the interest in the *nomos* (the administration) of the *oikos.* However, a single-minded interest in the *nomos,* I realized, has the capacity to threaten the very well-being of the *oikos,* or even, perhaps, its sustained existence. As a theological metaphor, *oikos* reminds us that history is bound up with community, webs of relationships, belonging, and life together. The *oikos* is a God-given space for living. It enables relationship, evokes neighborliness and living for the other, rather than for mere greed and self-interest.

The Hebrew Bible is underpinned by the notion of the *oikos.*[23] A critical engagement with the notion of "covenant" convinced me that, as a basic notion or referential category for faith, the divide in the history of the interpretation of the notion needs to be overcome between those who see the covenant as something to be "cut" between two equal, this-worldly partners, and others who regard it as God's initiative and gift, which can only be received in grace. Covenant is both a noun and a verb. It deals with who we are and how we act. The Bible is specifically alert when vulnerable life is at stake. It is precisely from here that the idea of God as the God of the helpless evolved. This is how we came to know God as the God "who supports the downtrodden, protects the stranger, helps orphans."[24]

When we speak of life in relation to global economic realities, we should focus on the status of vulnerable life in the system. The immediacy of the relationship between God and humanity is nowhere more profoundly expressed than in the idea of the covenant. In God's covenant, humanity and the earth are

23. The New Testament breathes the centrality of the keyword. It opens with the claim that, in Jesus Christ, God dwells among the people. Where the Spirit is present, the group becomes a household. This keyword also opens up a new status for the children of God: from being slaves to being free persons, sons and daughters. They eat a common meal in the *oikos.* They pray together for that common meal. The first church is depicted as a household of life, sharing, and cooperation. Again, the weakest, the exploited, and the poorest are preciously protected within the household.

24. The Belhar Confession is available online at http://www.pcusa.org.

embraced and addressed by the promises of a loving God. In the connection covenant-creation we learn that humanity is created for relationship with God. Every human being shares that relationship equally with other members of humankind. When that relationship is intact, humanity's existential interactions, contracts, treaties, and communities are authentic. Human beings now represent God in the care of covenantal living in creation and in the economy. Covenantal acts and covenanting beings manifest the integration of the discourses of equality (covenant and creation), reconciliation (covenant and re-creation), and *oikos* (covenant and life).

How is all of this connected with the relation of globalization to the *kairos* of dread and the *kairos* of hope? I became convinced that the crucial theological discourse in the context of economic globalization is the *oikos* discourse. With Enrique Dussel I believe that the very essence of ethical community, reflected in the holistic world of the biblical *oikos*, is under attack in the context of economic globalization.[25] What is at stake is the Christian faith or affirmation that God, who created this world in covenantal relationships, continues to sustain it and its living organisms.

Polish sociologist Zygmunt Bauman refers to a state of the human being amidst economic globalization that is geared towards tourists' dreams and desires rather than those of the poorest locals.[26] Economic globalization, he claims, produces two human forms, the tourist and the vagabond. The tourists are those human beings with the means and ability to choose to travel because they want to do so. The vagabonds are involuntary tourists forced to travel because they have no other bearable choice. The real lifeblood of a voluntary tourist is the possibility of choice. Globalization, Bauman claims, therefore is geared towards the dreams and desires of the tourist, not those of the vagabond. The latter are the poor and sidelined members of the human community. They represent the people living in the squatter camps of South Africa, the ghettos of the world. According to Bauman, the reduction of options marginalizes the vagabond from the central activity of economic globalization, namely the unfettered right to choose. The vagabond is seen as a flawed consumer and, as such, useless to and unwanted in the global economy. So they participate in crime as a negative expression of their desperate wish to become like the tourist. Eventually, the vagabond learns that the tourist is actually dreaming of a world without vagabonds. They therefore

25. E. D. Dussel, *Ethics and Community* (Maryknoll, NY: Orbis Books, 1988).

26. Z. Bauman, *Globalization: The Human Consequences* (New York: Columbia University Press, 2000).

choose secluded tourist destinations rather than spaces where the vagabonds wander the streets of the world.

Globalization includes and excludes peoples and countries by its very nature, by its particular set of preferences and penalties applied variously to those who engage with or challenge its forces. In essence, it fragments the *oikos* on the basis of a particular *nomos* (law) that takes precedence over the community. This is the dread we have to overcome.

From *Kairoi* of Dread to *Kairoi* of Dreams

The idea of an African Dream will not be something foreign to you. After all, the United States is the birthplace of the famous concept of the *American* Dream. You may also be familiar with historian Jim Cullen's 2003 publication, *The American Dream: A Short History of an Idea That Shaped a Nation.*[27] He calls the American Dream the most "immediate component of an American identity, a birth right far more meaningful and compelling than terms like 'democracy,' 'Constitution,' or even 'the United States.'"[28] According to Cullen, the phrase itself, though implicit in the views of the Pilgrims and Founding Fathers, is less than a century old. In the forbidding and turbulent atmosphere of the Great Depression in 1931, historian James Trunslow Adams published *The Epic of America* and coined the phrase "the American Dream" as a "better, richer, and happier life for all our citizens of every rank, which is the greatest contribution we have made to the thought and welfare of the world. That dream or hope has been present from the start."[29]

27. J. Cullen, *The American Dream: A Short History of an Idea That Shaped a Nation* (Oxford: Oxford University Press, 2004).

28. Jon Meacham, "Keeping the Dream Alive," *Time,* Thursday, June 21, 2012. Online at http://www.content.time.com.

29. J. D. Adams, *The Epic of America* (Boston: Little, Brown, 1933). According to Cullen, although the list of possible interpretations of this dream is almost inexhaustible, it may be narrowed down thus: (1) the original American Dream, small groups of religious English dissenters who traversed an ocean seeking a way of worshiping God as they saw fit; (2) "the charter of the American Dream," the Declaration of Independence; (3) the most familiar American Dream, that of upward mobility, a dream typically understood in terms of economic and/or social advancement; (4) "one of the most noteworthy — and unsuccessful — of all American Dreams, the quest for equality, focusing specifically on the struggle of African Americans"; (5) the most widely realized American Dream, that of home ownership; and (6) a "dream of personal fulfilment." As with the other manifestations of the American Dream, this one also has a long history stretching back to the roots of American life, "[b]ut nowhere does this dream

It seems, though, that the American Dream, this very important social cement that holds together a nation (unlike that of other nations, like blood, language, shared religion, etc.), is coming apart. Cullen says, "[i]n some ways, large transnational institutions like corporations shape the lives of ordinary citizens far more than local government does. Economic and racial stratification have grown markedly, raising doubts about the breadth and depth of opportunity."

According to Frank A. Thomas:

> Dating back to the mid-1980s, there has been a sense that the American Dream is slipping away. . . . Given the recent near collapse of our economic system, the taxpayer/government bailout of financial institutions thought heretofore to be virtually invincible, painfully high unemployment and the persistent jobless recovery, one-quarter of American homes "underwater," such that people owe more than the home is worth, the expansive and expanding economic gap between the rich, middle and permanent underclass, the inability of the political system to offer any relevant solutions, the nagging effects of globalization, and the increasing sense that the nation is moving in the wrong direction, there is a hue and cry across the land as to whether the American Dream can deliver "a better, richer, and happier life for all our citizens of every rank."[30]

I leave it to you to judge the state of the contemporary American Dream, but I want to concur with Cullen that "[i]n the 19th and 20th centuries, no one spoke of the French Dream or the Russian Dream, but in the 21st century"

---

come more vividly into focus than in the culture of Hollywood — a semi-mythic place where, unlike in the Dream of Upward Mobility, fame and fortune were all the more compelling if achieved without obvious effort. This is the most alluring and insidious of American Dreams, and one that seems to have become predominant at the start of the twenty-first century."

30. Frank A. Thomas, *American Dream 2.0: A Christian Way Out of the Great Recession* (Nashville: Abingdon, 2012), xii. One of the challenges Thomas identifies in relation to the American Dream is that it "has come to be exclusively defined from a materialistic perspective, with economic benefit its chief aim and the primary measure of human happiness." This view is shared by many, including Ted Ownby, who writes about the change from the American Dream to "the four dreams of consumerism" in contemporary American society: the "Dream of Abundance" (which made America the richest society on earth); the "Dream of the Democracy of Goods" (the pursuit of access to the same goods regardless of race, gender, class or ethnicity); the "Dream of Freedom of Choice" (the pursuit of choice in the light of the ever-expanding variety of goods); and the "Dream of Novelty" (the pursuit of ever-changing fashions and new products). Ted Ownby, *American Dreams in Mississippi: Consumers, Poverty, and Culture, 1830-1998* (Chapel Hill: University of North Carolina Press, 1999).

the idea of the Dream has spread globally.[31] According to Emily S. Rosenburg, in "a vision of global social progress," the overseas version of the American Dream of "liberal-developmentalism" was born.[32] In short, despite this terminology, what this meant in *Africa* was an African Dream of economic growth and prosperity.

The Primacy of Hope: Revisiting the African Dream

So, what could possibly be wrong with a dream of economic growth for Africa? In fact, some would argue that it is exactly here that the hope of Africa lies and where it is already found. Africa is increasingly being identified as a success story — albeit a qualified one. Analysts have noted that "a new wave of optimism"[33] is sweeping across the continent, and the international discourse is changing "from Afro-pessimism to Afro-optimism."[34]

However, optimism devoid of true hope is flawed. Is economic growth and prosperity necessarily the answer? Not if it is built on a global model of exclusion instead of inclusion, competition instead of cooperation, fragmentation instead of cohesion, enrichment for a few and grinding poverty for the rest.

And then there are the concerns of sustainability; the need to go the "green economy" route looms as large for Africa as it does for the rest of the world, as pointed out recently by Swilling:

> Africa . . . will be forced to choose: it can either try to follow the same pathway to prosperity as the developed world, or it can strive to achieve its

31. Meacham, "Keeping the Dream Alive."

32. Emily S. Rosenburg, *Spreading the American Dream: American Economic and Cultural Expansion 1890-1945* (New York: Hill and Wang, 1982), 22-23, 7. This has five elements: "(1) the belief that other nations could and should replicate America's own developmental experience; (2) faith in private free enterprise; (3) support for free or open access for trade and investment; (4) promotion of free flow of information and culture; and (5) growing acceptance of governmental activity to protect private enterprise and to stimulate and regulate American participation in international economic and cultural exchange."

33. M. Swilling, "Africa 2050: Growth, Resource Productivity and Decoupling," policy brief for the seventh meeting of the International Panel for Sustainable Resource Management of the United Nations Environment Program, Stellenbosch, South Africa, 2010. Available online at http://www.learndev.org.

34. Scarlett Cornelissen, "The Start of History? The Promises and Limitations of Emerging Vectors in Africa's Political Economy," Stellenbosch University inaugural address, 2011. Available online at http://hdl.handle.net/10019.1/86798.

> developmental goals by finding a pathway that is not resource and energy intensive. If it opts for the former, it will gradually end up lagging behind the rest of the world technologically because many other countries (in particular Europe and China) are rapidly advancing by investing in resource productivity and energy efficiency. If it opts for the latter, it will need to invest in human capital and technological innovation on an unprecedented scale. Indeed, there is already evidence that the most significant contributors to African growth are economies that are diversifying by doing just this. The challenge is how far is Africa prepared to go towards the building of rapidly growing green economies.[35]

The challenge is global, and my argument is also informed by other theological views as well as non-theological views. For the latter, one may start by heeding the warning by 1700 of the world's leading scientists. Back in 1992 already they declared:

> Human beings and the natural world are on a collision course. Human activities inflict harsh and often irreversible damage on the environment and on critical resources. If not checked, many of our current practices put at serious risk the future that we wish for human society and the plant and animal kingdoms, and may so alter the living world that it will be unable to sustain life in the manner that we know. Fundamental changes are urgent if we are to avoid the collision our present course will bring about.[36]

One can also look at the warning expressed eleven years later by James Wolfensohn, then president of the World Bank:

> It is time to take a cold, hard look at the future. Our planet is not balanced. Too few control too much, and many have too little to hope for. Too much turmoil, too many wars, too much suffering. The demographics of the future speak to a growing imbalance of people, resources, and the environment. If we act together now, we can change the world for the better. If we do not, we shall leave greater and more intractable problems for our children.[37]

35. Swilling, "Africa 2050."

36. Quoted by R. Jensen, "The Anguish in the American Dream," *Common Dreams*, 2011. Available online at https://www.commondreams.org.

37. James D. Wolfensohn, Address to the Board of Governors of the World Bank Group, September 23, 2003. Quoted in Jensen, "The Anguish in the American Dream."

Hope that is driven primarily by economic growth and structure has the potential to lead to false hope. According to the American organizational theorist and pioneer in the field of operations research, systems thinking, and management science, Russell L. Ackoff, growth is not the same as development, and neither presupposes the other:

> Rubbish heaps grow but do not develop. . . . Some nations grow larger without developing and others develop without growing. Growth is an increase in size or number. Development is an increase in competence, the ability to satisfy one's needs and desires and those of others. Growth is a matter of earning; development is a matter of learning. Standard of living is an index of national growth; quality of life is an index of its development. Development is not a matter of how much one has but how much one can do with whatever one has.[38]

We should be living as if the values of a society, the worth of a person, and the integrity of the planet define true hope. This stems from the insight that the future defines the present and its ethical responsibility. Globally, we are again facing a juncture of dread and hope.

From African Dream to Global Dream: How Do We Live, and For Whom Do We Live?

At the juncture of dread and hope that we are now facing, in Africa and globally, we are also faced with the problem of the future, something that has always been a challenge to Christian thought. In fact, it has always been, I believe, the most fundamental confessional quest in Christianity. It demands of us to live in a certain way, to live ethically, to live in hope. What does this mean?

Again, I believe, we should return to the Bible, perhaps to another chapter in 1 Corinthians, to what has been called by some theologians the key to Christian ethics, or, in the words of Cullmann, the "most outright expression" of the ethical principle of Paul:[39]

38. Russell L. Ackoff, "Transforming the Systems Movement," opening speech at the Third International Conference on Systems Thinking in Management (ICSTM '04), Philadelphia, May 19, 2004. Available online at http://www.acasa.upenn.edu.

39. For an exegesis of this passage, see H. R. Botman and D. J. Smit, "Exegesis and Proclamation: 1 Corinthians 7:29-31, 'To live . . . as if it were not!'" *Journal of Theology for Southern Africa* 65 (1988): 73-79.

> What I mean, brothers and sisters, is that the time is short. From now on those who have wives should live as if they do not; those who mourn, as if they did not; those who are happy, as if they were not; those who buy something, as if it were not theirs to keep; those who use the things of the world, as if not engrossed in them. For this world in its present form is passing away. (1 Cor. 7:29-31)

A detailed discussion of this text is not possible here, save to make the following brief observations. Our ethical stance vis-à-vis the status quo is based on the realization that there is nothing absolute or definitive about the status quo, because "the form of this world is passing." Christian eschatology, which this text is all about, has a distinctive ethical effect in that it leads to a "critical-realism" with regard to the world. At the same time it invalidates any absolutism with regard to the status quo, because it relativizes all the schemes of this present order. This very same eschatology will also be the regulator of the attitudes and conducts that will militate against absolutism and facilitate the radical dismantling thereof. This is the eschatology that will "undemonize the world."[40] And, while the future of God cannot be brought about by the lifestyle of Christians, this lifestyle nevertheless must necessarily reflect God's future.[41] For Christians, whatever exists is continually relativized by that which *can* be and that which *must* be and that which undoubtedly *shall* be. In short, Christian eschatology allows us — no, forces us — to hope, to dream, and indeed to live "as if" the status quo "is not."

Furthermore, we have to ask for whom we are hoping, for whom we are to live in hope. We hope for ourselves, of course, but even more importantly, for the next generations. We have to live in an economically and ecologically responsible way with regard to our planet — after all, as is often heard in contemporary ecological discourse, we are indeed not the owners of our world, but only the stewards of it on behalf of our children. But this is only one of the elements of the despair faced by the next generation, by the youth of our world, by those on whose behalf we too have to live, hope, and dream. They dread not only the state of the environment we live in but also the kind of society we find ourselves in.

40. P. Wendland, *Die urchristlichen Literaturformen*, HNT 1.3 (Tübingen: J. C. B. Mohr, 1912).

41. It was this eschatologically imprinted ethic that was developed in terms of a politically inspired "praxis of hope" by so-called political theologians. Where others would say that Christian eschatology calls for tolerative moderation, the political theologies suggest that it warrants direct critical action for socio-political change.

In 1976 the youth of South Africa stood up in the midst of their dread of an apparently hopeless future. These were one of the signs of the times that were discerned in the streets, homes, and churches of South Africa in those days. In the Kairos Document and in the Belhar Confession we dreamed and hoped and acted on behalf of the despondent youth of our beleaguered country. The youth of today dread much more complex things; they need the guidance and the values of Belhar, but in a time that demands much more of them.[42] Today, the dread is not confined to the youth of the southernmost tip of a forgotten continent; today the dread we and our youth face reaches all corners of the world. A dread of a hopeless future, similar to that experienced by the South African youth of decades ago, is now shared by the global youth. In a sense I find myself once more as I was in the classroom at the University of the Western Cape in 1978, now in a vastly different time, facing a different kind of dread, looking for hope, dreaming — no longer for myself as a young person, but *for* young people, as I was then. It is indeed time to act upon the appeal of the Accra Document, to discern the signs of the times, and of the Kitwe Statement, to see, judge, and act, to realize "[o]ur people's dreams and hopes of social equality, political freedom and economic justice," and to see that all that is ecologically, economically, and in this sense morally wrong with our world, is having "disastrous repercussions on future generations."[43]

We should indeed heed the appeal of Wolfensohn to "take a cold hard look at the future." This is our task as Africans, but also that of you, my American hosts, and of people worldwide. If we do not carry out this task, the global youth may find their only hope in extreme rightwing or leftist anarchical groups. We must dream a new dream, a new African and Global Dream, wary of the trappings of the American Dream that your fellow countrymen have pointed out to us. Instead of pursuing industrialization, we should think first of what is best for the planet; and instead of concentrating on individualism, we should not forget that we reside in a global community.

The calling of Christians, especially Reformed believers, is to problematize the future so that the next generation can inherit a world that better resembles the will of God. We have the responsibility to leave a legacy of hope.

42. Cf. H. R. Botman, foreword to *Good News to Confess: The Belhar Confession and the Road of Acceptance* by J. Botha and P. Naudé (Wellington, SA: Bible Media, 2010), 7-8.

43. Kitwe Statement, paragraphs 3 and 8.

Acting on Hope in a Secular Context

In my current position as Rector and Vice-Chancellor of Stellenbosch University, I have tried to dream with our students and staff a new dream, to hope anew. For me this was partly a personal appeal to people everywhere to confess hope — religiously to the religious, secularly in a secular context.

In my installation address in 2007, I highlighted the work of Brazilian educator Paulo Freire.[44] He had argued that education should help change the world for the better by stimulating a critical consciousness in the face of oppression, poverty, injustice and the difficult task of living peacefully with former oppressors in a post-conflict situation. I reminded my colleagues that Stellenbosch University had already in the year 2000 taken the important step of acknowledging that it had contributed to the injustices of South Africa's apartheid past.[45] Significantly, the University had expressed a commitment to "redress," which it said it would pursue through "equity" in the form of broadening access by people from groups which had in the past been excluded, and through "service" in the form of promoting development in communities and areas previously disadvantaged in the provisioning of services and infrastructure. I said I was dedicating my time in office to the realization of this commitment, and proposed that we follow a "pedagogy of hope" to this end.

Following broad consultation and engagement, the University subsequently formally adopted hope as its "guiding concept," undertaking to "creat[e] hope in and from Africa by means of excellent scholarly practice."[46] The institution explained that this leads it to "ask critical questions about reality, to look at problems in a scientific manner and to use science to make a difference" under the "assumption that another and better reality can and must be created and cultivated by creating, applying and sharing new knowledge." This step found practical expression in Stellenbosch University's HOPE Project,[47] through which the institution's core activities — research, teaching, and community interaction — have been focused on eradicating poverty and

44. The address can be found online at http://hdl.handle.net/10019.1/21165. See particularly P. Freire, *Pedagogy of the Oppressed* (1970; London: Penguin, 1996), and *Pedagogy of Hope: Reliving Pedagogy of the Oppressed* (1992; London: Continuum, 2004).

45. In its "Strategic Framework for the Turn of the Century and Beyond," available online at www.sun.ac.za/university/stratplan/statengels.doc.

46. "Hope as Guiding Concept for Stellenbosch University," available online at http://hdl.handle.net/10019.1/80686.

47. More information at www.thehopeproject.co.za.

related conditions, contributing to human dignity and health, consolidating democracy and human rights, promoting peace and security, and balancing a sustainable environment with a competitive industry in South Africa and the rest of the continent. Consequently, "creating hope" has become "the reason why this University exists."[48]

Conclusion

Theologically speaking, I have brought you a testimony, not a new thought in theology. I have stuck to a familiar central message, only repositioned contextually. And that has been to pay attention to the plight of the global youth experience; to read the signs of our times; to study and heed the long-term implications of our short- and medium-term "solutions"; and to understand the nature of the sacrifices we are asked to make.

Finally, for us as Christians, this is closely related to the question about to whom we belong. Today we indeed seem to "belong" to entities beyond ourselves — to the global economic system. We are citizens of a global village, and the majority of us are second-rate citizens at that, living on its margins. Of course we should belong. Ubuntu, Africa's "small gift to the world"[49] (meaning that "my humanity is caught up and inextricably bound up in yours. . . . I am because I belong"), is exactly about this. However, in a much more profound way, Calvin confesses in Book III of his *Institutes of the Christian Religion* that "we belong not to ourselves, but to God in Jesus Christ." We belong in kairotic relationship and in covenantal time. From this perspective we may dream a new dream for Africa and for the rest of the world. From this perspective, we, in the words of Desmond Tutu, may hear God say:

> I have a dream. . . . Please help Me to realize it. It is a dream of a world whose ugliness and squalor and poverty, its war and hostility, its greed and harsh competitiveness, its alienation and disharmony are changed into their glorious counterparts, when there will be more laughter, joy, and peace, where there will be justice and goodness and compassion and love and caring and sharing. I have a dream that swords will be beaten into plowshares and spears into pruning hooks, that My children will know that they are

48. "Hope as Guiding Concept for Stellenbosch University," available at http://hdl.handle.net/10019.1/80686.

49. Desmond Tutu, quoted in Botman, "The *Oikos* in a Global Economic Era: A South African Comment," in Cochrane and Klein, eds., *Sameness and Difference.*

> members of one family, the human family, God's family, My family. In God's family, there are no outsiders. All are insiders . . . all belong.[50]

This is my dream too, my hope, and I trust also yours. I see the recognition of my work in theology and public life through the Abraham Kuyper Prize as an expression of our common hope for a better future in the interest of the next generation — one that will know by hearsay, not only apartheid, but also the current global economic crisis.

50. D. Tutu with D. Abrams, *God Has a Dream: A Vision of Hope for Our Time* (Johannesburg: Rider, 2004), 19-20.

F. W. J. Schelling: A Philosophical Influence on Kuyper's Social Thought

Dylan Pahman

Introduction

That Abraham Kuyper was aware of F. W. J. Schelling's metaphysics is certain. Not only would he likely have encountered Schelling during his university studies at Leiden[1] and as a young modernist before his conversion to traditional Calvinism (Young 1952: 43-44; Heslam 1998: 29-35), but even after, he seems to have remained familiar with Schelling's metaphysics, if only to reject it. In a discussion of pantheism, he writes (Kuyper 1893: 521),

> Let us call it once more a spiritual adultery; but it is the glow of a tragic passion, which is far more attractive and captivating than the cold egotism of the matter-of-fact man, who may not question the existence of God, but has no further dealings with him than *pro memoria.* And also in our age it is noteworthy how the newly aroused Christian religion in Schleiermacher has kissed the hand of pantheism, and how Schelling (provided that the theistic name be retained) has allowed himself deep draughts from the foaming cup of pantheism. True piety shrank back from the rationalistic coldness

1. Eglinton (2010: 59) writes, "Prior to the Groningen school's development, the works of Kant, Fichte, and Schelling were largely ignored [in the Netherlands]. Schleiermacher became known in the 1830s, initially with very little impact. However, developments in Groningen and then Leiden brought considerable change." Again, more summarily, Eglinton (2012: 161) writes that "post-Enlightenment theology existed in a [sic] somewhat of a timelag in the Netherlands" and that "it took the writings of Kant, Hegel, Fichte, Schelling and Schleiermacher a considerable time to gain influence among Dutch intellectuals."

> and from the conventional mechanism of our supranaturalists. But at the hand of Schelling it regains its mysteries, its holy Trinity, its Incarnation, including even the doctrine of the resurrection.[2]

Kuyper (1893: 537) later notes in the same work that according to none other than Jan Hendrik Scholten, Kuyper's modernist professor at the University of Leiden, Schelling was responsible for "inspiring [the German idealists] . . . with the art of proclaiming 'new and strange ideas in ecclesiastical terms as the decisions of ancient orthodoxy.' "[3] While it must be admitted that Schelling appears to be the height of the modern pantheistic tendency according to Kuyper, these assessments of Schelling's metaphysics can only be said to be praiseworthy relative to authors for whom Kuyper has an even lower assessment. Kuyper (1893: 537) goes on to say, "[L]et us grant that they jumped after the drowning man in the philosophic stream to save him; but the tragic fate overtook them of being dragged down by him whom they tried to save." Thus, it is quite understandable if, on this basis, one would reject offhand the idea that Schelling had any significant influence on Kuyper.

However, this paper argues the contrary. It should be noted that, in distinction from Veenhof, who argued that the organic motif in Kuyper and Bavinck derived in part from Schelling, and who, as Eglinton (2010: 54-58)[4] notes, was criticized by Caroline van Eck for failing to account for the history of organicism and by Mattson (2012: 47-54) for ultimately falling victim to

2. Kuyper seems somewhat hesitant to flatly label Schelling a pantheist, despite bemoaning the adverse influence pantheism had on Schelling's thought, in his view. Recently, Cooper (2006: 94-105) has examined Schelling's metaphysics in the context of a study on panentheism. The term *panentheism* was still not commonplace at the time Kuyper was writing. As Cooper (2006: 26), acknowledging its origin with Karl Krause, notes, "The term *panentheism* did not come into common usage, however, until Charles Hartshorne popularized it in the mid-twentieth century."

3. For a brief account of Scholten's thought, see Young 1952: 37-39. Notably, while generally characterizing Scholten as an idealist, Young (1952: 39) writes, "It is not difficult to detect in the background of Scholten's theology, the philosophy of Spinoza." A synthesis of Spinoza and idealism, for the purpose of theodicy, is precisely Schelling's project in *Of Human Freedom,* as will be detailed below. However, Scholten's determinism, in contrast to Schelling, is well attested. See Eglinton 2010: 59-63 and 2012: 132-38. Much of the former article (Eglinton 2010) also reappears in chapter 3 of Eglinton 2012: 51-80. Eglinton also classifies Scholten's thought as both mechanism and idealism, while attributing organicism to both Hegel and Schelling.

4. Notably, Eglinton focuses exclusively on Bavinck and convincingly argues against the theses of Veenhof in the case of Bavinck, though he does not address Kuyper in any detail. See also Eglinton 2012: 51-80.

the genetic fallacy, my thesis does not depend on any close correspondence of vocabulary at all. Nevertheless, it is worth noting that Bratt (2013: 185-86) has recently linked Kuyper to Schelling's organicism partly (but not solely) on the basis of common vocabulary, writing in the context of Kuyper's distinction between the Church as organism and as institution.

> [D]rawing on the nature-philosophy of Friedrich Schelling, [the new set of philosophical concepts] could link any number of diverse elements as the "expression" of an "organism" that "developed" from a single "root" by its internal "law" (or "principle") toward its inherent end. The words in quotation marks appear endlessly in Kuyper's work, including his ecclesiology, perhaps making Schelling the instrument by which he could finally reconcile Schleiermacher and Calvin.[5]

Bratt's assessment, at the very least, merits a closer look at the possible influence of Schelling's philosophy on Kuyper's social thought.

In particular, I argue that the structure of their narratives of autonomy — for Schelling in metaphysics and for Kuyper in relation to the historical emergence of sovereign spheres — approaches a formal identity, and that this correspondence of such a unique formal structure must be more than coincidental. I demonstrate this by examining and comparing the former in Schelling's *Of Human Freedom* (originally published in 1809) and the latter with respect to the sphere of art in *Wisdom & Wonder: Common Grace in Science & Art* (originally published in 1905), each on their own terms and only later comparing them. Accordingly, this paper consists of three sections: In the first, I outline Schelling's metaphysics in *Of Human Freedom*. In the second, I outline Kuyper's account of how art developed historically into its own sovereign sphere and the necessity that it be submitted to the sovereign rule of Jesus Christ, that it still be sacred though independent of the sacred realm of the Church, in *Wisdom & Wonder*. Having explicated the foregoing, I conclude by arguing for the influence of the formal structure of Schelling's metaphysics on Kuyper's signature doctrine of sphere sovereignty.

5. Kuyper's sermon in which he sets out the distinction between the Church as institution and organism is now available in English. See Kuyper 2013.

Schelling

Shelling begins his work *Of Human Freedom* by articulating the immense difficulty of rationally justifying both freedom and necessity.[6] "Without the contradiction of necessity and freedom," he (Schelling 1936: 9) writes, "not only philosophy but every nobler ambition of the spirit would sink to that death which is peculiar to those sciences in which that contradiction serves no function." What is one to do? Should philosophy and "every nobler ambition of the spirit" simply be abandoned? Not according to Schelling (1936: 9): "To withdraw from the conflict [between freedom and necessity] by foreswearing reason looks more like flight than victory."

This contradiction, according to Schelling (1936: 9-10), can be "pointedly expressed in the sentence: Pantheism is the only possible system of reason but is inevitably fatalism." Thus he delves into an examination of Spinoza, pantheist *par excellence.* Interestingly, he clearly views Spinoza as a panentheist rather than a pantheist, by the current uses of the terms: "a more complete differentiation of things and God can hardly be conceived than is made in the teaching of Spinoza which is said to be the classic instance of its identification" (Schelling 1936: 11-12).[7] For Schelling (1936: 12), Spinoza (and thus pantheism) is best viewed as the belief that "God is that which is in itself and is conceived solely through itself; whereas the finite necessarily exists in another being and can only be conceived with reference to it." Shelling (1936: 22) will later differentiate his system from Spinoza's, stating,

> Here, then, once and for all our definite opinion about Spinozism! This system is not fatalism because it lets things be conceived in God; . . . pantheism does not make formal freedom, at least, impossible. Spinoza must then be fatalist for another reason, entirely independent of this. The error in his system is by no means due to the fact that he posits all *things in God,* but to the fact that they are *things* — to the abstract conception of the world and its creatures, indeed of eternal Substance itself, which is also a thing for him.

Their static reality as things is, according to Schelling, the reason why all things are bound by fate to Spinoza, not the fact that all are derived from and are in God.

6. For a more detailed summary of Schelling's *Of Human Freedom,* see White 1983: 106-45. See also Marx 1984: 58-85.

7. Cooper (2006: 71-72) notes that there remains debate today whether Spinoza was a pantheist or panentheist, himself endorsing the former view.

From there he turns to the German idealists, a label which, to him, signifies primarily Kant and Fichte. Idealism identified Being with unbounded, self-affirming Will. Thus, "we owe to it," writes Schelling (1936: 24), "the first formally perfect concept of freedom." Despite this praise, he continues, "However . . . Idealism itself is, after all, nothing less than a finished system. And as soon as we seek to enter into the doctrine of freedom in greater detail and exactitude, it nonetheless leaves us helpless." Neither Spinozism nor German idealism have been sufficient to rationally grasp the essence and origin of real freedom. A synthesis is therefore in order.

For Schelling (1936: 26), "the real and vital conception of freedom," in distinction from the formal definition of idealism, "is that it is a possibility of good and evil."[8] However, for a realist system (in the sense of Spinozism or pantheism) this immediately raises the question of theodicy. If all is derived from and is in God, and we do in fact have freedom, then is not at least the possibility of evil and therefore the realization of evil in the world attributable to God in some way? Schelling is determined to answer no. To do so, he posits a very odd metaphysic. For the purposes of this paper, I must omit a vital part of it, his understanding of indifference as the groundless (Schelling 1936: 86-91). By no means, however, do I intend to imply that it is unimportant to Schelling's metaphysics and theodicy; it is simply unimportant to this study.

The solution to the problem of evil can be achieved, according to Schelling (1936: 86), through the "distinction between being insofar as it is basis, and being insofar as it exists."[9] God is being insofar as it exists while "the depth"

8. For an interesting exploration of human, moral freedom in Schelling as what distinguishes humanity from other animals, see Wirth 2005: 84-100.

9. Heidegger (1985: 107) summarizes these terms in Schelling as follows: " 'Being' *(Wesen)* is not meant here in the sense of the 'essence' of a thing, but in the sense in which we speak of a 'living being,' of 'household affairs,' of educational matters. What is meant is the individual, self-contained being as a whole." " 'Ground' always means for Schelling foundation, substratum, 'basis,' thus not 'ground' in the sense of 'ratio,' not with the counterconcept 'consequence' insofar as the *ratio* says why a statement is true or not true." He goes on to emphasize that "ground" for Schelling is nonrational, but not irrational. " 'Existence' does not really mean the manner of Being; but, rather, beings themselves in a certain regard — as existing; as we speak of a dubious 'existence' and mean the existing person himself. Schelling uses the word existence in a sense which is closer to the literal etymological sense than the usual long prevalent meaning of 'existing' as objective presence. Ex-sistence, *what emerges from itself* and in *emerging reveals itself*." He concludes, "From this explanation: 'ground' as what forms the substratum, 'existence' as what reveals itself, it can already be seen that this distinction by no means coincides with a current one in philosophy: that of *essentia* and *existentia*, 'essence' and 'existence,' what-ness and that-ness."

or darkness is being as the basis of realization. The first mode of being corresponds to the idealistic, the second to the Spinozistic. The will of God (being as existence) is to reveal (or realize) itself. It is not, in itself, revealed. The will of the depths (being as basis) or the darkness (or matter or nature) is to exist. It does not, in itself, exist. The former is actuality and the latter is potentiality. It is in the combination of the two that the world comes to be. God, willing out of love to reveal himself, differentiates from the darkness the seed of light which is present within it as potentiality. Light is born from the darkness as its basis. This light is God revealing or realizing himself. Inasmuch as the darkness wills to exist, the act is a loving one: God is imparting existence to the darkness by transfiguring it into light.

Nevertheless, when the will of the darkness to exist is exalted above rather than subordinate to the light, when it becomes the will to exist *for itself*, then evil arises as the basis for conscious spirit.[10] This evil is not yet "bad" inasmuch as it is the necessary "container" for the revelation of the good, which comes about when the now conscious spirit, through love, subordinates itself once again to the light. According to Schelling (1936: 50), "every nature can be revealed only in its opposite — love in hatred, unity in strife. If there were no division of the principles, then unity could not manifest its omnipotence; if there were no conflict then love could not become real." Love divides the light from the darkness in order that the darkness might exist as light. The primal unity is only one of potential existence. The final unity is one of actualized existence and realized revelation, "that God may be all in all" (Schelling 1936: 86).

I now move to Schelling's anthropology. "Man has been placed," Schelling (1936: 50) writes,

> on that summit where he contains within him the source of self-impulsion towards good and evil in equal measure; the nexus of the principles within him is not a bond of necessity but of freedom. He stands at the dividing line; whatever he chooses will be his act, but he cannot remain in indecision because God must necessarily reveal himself and because nothing at all in creation can remain ambiguous.

10. According to Heidegger (1985: 143), "[E]vil proclaims itself as a position of will of its own, indeed as a way of being free in the sense of being a self in terms of its own essential law. By elevating itself above the universal will, the individual will wants precisely to be that will. Through this elebation a way of unification of its own takes place, thus a way of its own of being Spirit." For more on freedom and evil in this connection, see White 1983: 124-31. On freedom and evil in Schelling's thought more broadly, see Fackenheim 1996: 95-99.

The cause of man's temptation is precisely the will of the depths asserting itself to exist for itself, the evil out of which he achieved selfhood, becoming a free, conscious spirit capable of good and evil. This, however, is the necessary conflict for the realization of love through the union of the will of love and the will of the depths, subordinated to the light rather than for itself, at this point an act of self-renunciation.[11] It is only in this way that God can reveal himself as person and that all things can exist in love.

When man subordinates his spirit to the light through love, the good that existed only potentially in the evil from which his spirit was born becomes actualized while the truly evil is suppressed to the point of pure potentiality or nonexistence. Thus, in the eschaton a certain pantheism results in which all is united in love. Light and darkness are united inasmuch as light eternally will exist in actuality and darkness for darkness (i.e., evil) only in potentiality. That is, evil will not properly exist at all. The darkness will be united to the light and identified with it inasmuch as the light arises from it and the light that was in it *in potentia* has been fully actualized through it while that which strove against love to exist for its own sake has been utterly suppressed (Schelling 1986: 89-90).

But what of evil? Has Schelling really solved the problem? He certainly thinks so:

> But whoever found in this final, highest viewpoint an identity of good and evil, would show his total ignorance, since evil and good in no way form an original antithesis, least of all a duality. There is a duality when there are really two beings which stand in opposition to one another. Evil, however, is no being but a counterfeit of being, which is real only by contrast, not in itself. Moreover, absolute identity, the spirit of love, is prior to evil just because the latter can only appear in contrast to it. Hence, too, it cannot be comprehended in absolute identity, but is rather excluded and banished from it eternally. (Schelling 1986: 90-91)[12]

11. According to Heidegger (1985: 136), "The ground . . . wants to be more and more ground, and at the same time it can only will this by willing what is clearer and thus striving *against itself* as what is dark."

12. It is significant to note that Schelling does not deny an antithesis between good and evil, only that such an antithesis is "original." In this point he is distinct from Hegel. Findlay (1977: 588) summarizes Hegel as follows: "That God becomes alienated from himself in angelic and human evil does not mean that such evil really lies outside of God. To be distant from God is to be distantly God: nothing can lie outside of the Absolute Being. . . . Evil is in a deep sense the same being-for-self as absolute good, yet, in a deeper sense, it is not the same, since in fully developed being-for-self evil will be set aside and overcome. The true selfishness will drive out the untrue. It is above all mistaken in this sphere to speak in terms of fixed identity

Evil, it must be remembered, only arose as the darkness strove against love to exist for itself. While this was necessary in order that spirit might be born in man, ultimately man freely must choose good over evil and triumph over evil through love. The spirit of love, the "absolute identity" by which the potential good in evil is actualized at the exclusion (or repression) of all potential evil in eternity, clearly cannot include an identity of good and evil, for evil has been triumphed over and excluded in order that the destiny of God, the will of love, might be fully accomplished and revealed.

Kuyper

In *Wisdom & Wonder,* Kuyper (2011: 116) writes that "so much of art with its diversity could [only] emerge at first like an ivy vine curling around the sacred, and only in a later stage of development grow into an entirely independent plant." Art, both pre-Christian and Christian, began its existence within the sacred.

Given the connection between the visual arts and idolatry in paganism, Kuyper asks whether the proper Christian response to visual art would be condemnation, but answers in the negative. "[I]s that the proper question?" Kuyper (2011: 116) asks,

> Or should we not rather acknowledge that in its initial appearance, art was powerless in learning to walk had it not been held by the reins of the priest? Should we not acknowledge that once it had achieved further development, art could appeal in every possible way to an independent, free, and autonomous existence?

Ancient and Medieval art, by his telling, was like a child that had not yet fully matured. The sacred realm — the Church in particular — acted like a parent,

---

and diversity, and to fail to recognize the dialectical movement which makes everything turn into something else. Nature is and is not God, and God is God only by departing from himself in Nature, and returning to himself in Spirit." See also Hegel 1977: 471-75 for Hegel's own account. By contrast, for Schelling, evil is being as basis asserting itself to exist in and for itself, apart from God and the light, i.e., apart from being as existence. As such it does not properly have existence and cannot be said to exist in the absolute or being as existence but only as a distortion or negation. The important difference comes precisely in Schelling's distinguishing between being as existence and being as basis; only the former is God to him, not the latter. For Hegel, Nature is God in a particular mode of existence, and evil is overcome by transfiguration, rather than by repression as for Schelling.

holding the hand of art until the time that it could walk on its own. According to Kuyper (2011: 177), "support needed to be provided to the spirit of the Christian religion as the only means for supplying the creation of Christian art. It was simply regrettable that this newborn art was too one-sided and too exclusively ecclesiastical." Kuyper (2011: 117) even goes so far as to say that this narrative applies to education as well: "In this connection we recall education with all its branches, an enterprise that initially among both pagans and Christians leaned upon and was supported by the sacred and the holy, but thereafter came to stand on its own legs, and only in that independent position developed its proper essence."

While Kuyper (1998: 467) elsewhere states that Christian education first gained its independence at a much earlier time, according to him art remained within the sacred until the Reformation. Kuyper (2011: 119) writes,

> Only this much we admit, namely, that in its beginning stages, the course of the Reformation did cause disorder and confusion. The generation of that time, because it was accustomed to finding art mainly in the church building, and because it was driven to opposition out of spiritual aversion toward this art in the churches, risked the very serious peril after the churches were purified of condemning art as such. This peril was partially realized. At that time there was a certain aversion toward art that had arisen from a religious motive, a hostility that still continues to function in some circles even today. On the other hand, even less can it be denied that the art that had been newly set free entered all too quickly into the service of licentiousness and discarded its honor.[13]

13. While praising the freedom that art attained as a result of the Reformation, Schelling (1989: 70), too, admits the misfortune of "a certain aversion toward art that had arisen from a religious motive." For Schelling, that religious motive was an over-literalism and a misplaced dependence on human understanding. He writes, "Praise to the heroes who at that time [i.e., the Reformation], at least for certain parts of the world, eternally secured freedom of thought and of invention! The principle they awakened was fresh inspiration. Combined with the spirit of classical antiquity, it was able to generate infinite effects precisely because it really was infinite by *nature* and recognized no boundaries, though it was hindered anew by the misfortune of the age itself. . . . The slavery of the letter was even less able to endure, yet Protestantism was never really able to give itself an external and genuinely objective and finite form. Not only did it degenerate into sects, but what had been the retrieval of the eternal rights of the human spirit became a totally destructive principle both for religion and, indirectly, for poesy. What transpired was that peculiar elevation of common human understanding, the tool of merely worldly matters, to a position of judgment over spiritual matters." This, however, is a posthumous publication (1859) of Schelling's 1802 lectures on art at the University of Jena. Part of the introduction was published the next year (1803) in the section on art in his work *On University*

Kuyper does not think art should be condemned, nor does he think that it can exist for its own sake, wherein it is prone to enter "all too quickly into the service of licentiousness." Indeed, according to Heslam (1998: 197), "[Kuyper's] ideas [on art] ran counter to 'art for art's sake.'" In this context Kuyper (2011:179, see also 180-82) touches on the antithesis between the natural and the spiritual in art, writing,

> This [art for licentiousness] is the natural, which will continue in the context of sin until the end. As long as the mixture of the profane and the sacred persists on this earth, and the kingdom of glory, i.e., the highest ideal, is not yet realized, beauty cannot come to unity and harmonious manifestation. Within the world in which we dwell a multiform spirit exercises dominion, and in that spirit world the spirit of Christ and the spirit from below constitute opposing forces that are irreconcilable.

This antithesis is "irreconcilable." The solution is not a mixture of secularized or profane art with the sacred, but rather that art, freed from the realm of the sacred, would nevertheless remain sacred, affirming the sacred not only in the ecclesiastical, but in every realm of common life.

Indeed, despite the dangers he mentions, Kuyper (2011: 119) believes that the independence of art is a good thing, the result of a natural process, writing,

> [A]rt has been summoned to freedom. This claim is coupled with the insistence that in this way the separation between religion and art brought about by the Reformation was the inevitable effect of a natural process in a twofold sense. First, religion could confess its spiritual character only to the degree it was separated. And second, art could attain its rightful independence only to the degree it was separated.

Notably, in his *Lectures on Calvinism,* Kuyper (1931: 147-49) credits his understanding of this twofold natural process to Hegel and von Hartmann,[14] the latter of whose philosophy was itself significantly influenced by Schelling.[15]

Studies. See Schelling 1966: 143-52. As these lectures came before *Of Human Freedom,* they are not built directly upon the metaphysics of that work, which marks a development in Schelling's thought from his previous philosophy. Nevertheless, this passage has an interesting parallel with the above quote by Kuyper, even if only coincidentally.

14. This is also noted by Heslam 1998: 203-4. See also Heslam 1999: 17-18.

15. For example, in discussing the origin of consciousness, on the Becoming-Consciousness of the Idea, von Hartmann (1931: ii.91) credits Jacob Böhme and Schelling as being the first to articulate, albeit imperfectly, "an origin of consciousness from an opposition

However, the similarities with Hegel end there — formally, there is no similar threefold, thesis-antithesis-synthesis dialectic in Kuyper.[16] Furthermore, freedom is not bound up within a master-slave motif[17] nor with the concept of self-consciousness,[18] and art and religious history are not parts of the historical unfolding of the ethical or true Spirit.[19]

---

of different moments in the Unconscious." For a good, short study that more broadly explores von Hartmann's engagement with Schelling, among others, see Gardner 2010, esp. pp. 178-79 and 187-97.

16. See Hegel 1977: 119-38. For Hegel, first one posits one's self as *being-in-itself* (which he credits to Stoicism), then negates all that is alien to the self (which he credits to Skepticism), then resolves the inner duality that results from this by a third term, a "mediator" — the comparison of itself as negation of the *in-itself*, as nothing, to the Unchangeable, by which through self-renunciation and submission to universal will, one finds one's own action and being to be being and action *in themselves,* in which arises the idea of Reason for consciousness and the possibility of actual (rather than merely *in principle*) self-satisfaction and absolute action. Hegel (1977: 139) summarizes this as follows: "In grasping the thought that the *single* individual consciousness is *in itself* Absolute Essence, consciousness has returned into itself. For the Unhappy Consciousness [the negation of all otherness] the in-itself is the beyond of itself. But its movement has resulted in positing the completely developed single individual, or the single individual that is an *actual* consciousness, as the *negative* of itself, viz. as the *objective* extreme; in other words, it has successfully struggled to divest itself of its being-for-self and has turned into [mere] being. In this movement it has also become aware of its *unity* with this universal, a unity which, for us, no longer falls outside of it since the superseded single individual is the universal, and which, since consciousness maintains itself in this its negativity, is present in consciousness as such as its essence. Its truth is that which appears in the syllogism whose extremes appeared as held absolutely asunder, as the middle term which proclaims to the unchangeable consciousness that the single individual has renounced itself, and, to the individual, that the Unchangeable is for it no longer an extreme, but is reconciled with it. This middle term is the unity directly aware of both and connecting them, and is the consciousness of their unity, which it proclaims to consciousness and thereby to itself, the consciousness of the certainty of being all truth." That this bears no formal likeness to the development and purpose of sphere sovereignty in Kuyper's social thought should be obvious. For the dialectic to be the same the following would need to correspond in substance: sacred art and thesis, natural art and antithesis, spiritual art and synthesis. Yet, it is clear that despite some correspondence of vocabulary with Hegel (natural and antithesis, for example), art does not become spiritual by transforming the natural in synthesis with the sacred but by repressing the natural for the sacred. Rather than one unfolding Spirit, Kuyper acknowledges the malevolent working of "the spirit from below" against the Spirit of Christ as "opposing forces that are irreconcilable," as I have already noted above. For more on Hegel's dialectical method, see Forster 1993: 130-170, but especially pp. 131-133 for a basic overview.

17. See Hegel 1977: 111-19. See also Neuhouser 2009: 37-54.

18. See Hegel 1977: 119-38. See also Chiereghin 2009.

19. See Hegel 1977: 424-53. Findlay (1977: 586-87) has a helpful summary of the concept of Spirit for Hegel: "Spirit is essentially a process which starts from pure thought (logic), goes

For Kuyper, as Christianity more strongly embraced the call of Christ to "worship in spirit and truth" (John 4:24) in the Reformation, it needed to distance itself from the sensuality of the visual arts.[20] Art, for its part, was thereby set free to flourish once again as a sphere of common grace. As Kuyper (2011: 120) concludes,

> So, then, especially in the sixteenth century, art moved out of the tent of the sacred to erect its own tent in the domain of common grace, where it belongs. This was a phenomenon whose simultaneous consequence was that only when art was flourishing in the domain of common grace did it yearn for its significance to extend to all of human living in broader society.

Once freed, art longs to expand itself to every aspect of human life. And in so doing it is able to fulfill its proper role as a sphere of common grace. "In this way," Kuyper (2011: 178) writes,

> outside the church and freed from ecclesiastical domination, fresh artistic expression flourished at that point. Emerging from the classicism of ancient Greece under the leadership of the Renaissance and its return to nature, and owing its direct connection with popular culture to the Reformation, this fresh artistic expression opened up an entirely new period for the blossoming of art.

Today art exists in its proper place, as a sphere of common grace. It fulfills its calling when it suppresses the urge to exist for its own sake (or, for that matter, for immoral purposes) and when it further approaches the kingdom of glory by glorifying the work of the Spirit of God, active in every aspect of human life through common grace.

Schelling in and for Kuyper

Having taken the time to represent Schelling and Kuyper in their own terms, we can compare the formal structures of their narratives of autonomy as follows (Figure 1):

---

on into otherness and pictorial presentation (Nature), and returns from Nature to complete self-consciousness (Spirit proper). It is also essentially the synthetic connection of these three phases."

20. See Kuyper 2011: 178.

Figure 1: Comparison of the Formal Structure of F. W. J. Schelling's Metaphysics and Abraham Kuyper's Sphere Sovereignty

Formal Representation of Terms	Schelling	Kuyper
A	God	church
not-A	Darkness	art
A revealing itself in not-A	Light	sacred art
not-A asserting itself, in and for itself	darkness in and for itself	secularized art (i.e., art in and for itself)
not-A in itself for "A revealing itself in not-A" (i.e., for the revealed will of A)	darkness in itself for the light (i.e., conformed to God's will of love)	art in itself for the sacred (i.e., for the rule of Christ)

For Schelling, the darkness once existed only in the light as light. For Kuyper, art once existed only in the Church as sacred art. However, just as for Schelling darkness had to break free from the light to become autonomous, so also for Kuyper art had to break free from the Church to gain its proper independence among the spheres of common grace. Nevertheless, just as for Schelling the darkness, now existing in itself, cannot go on existing for itself but must freely subordinate itself to the light, so also for Kuyper art ought not to be wholly secularized but must exist for the sacred, lest it degenerate in licentiousness. Replace "the light" with "the sacred" and "the darkness" with "art" and Schelling becomes Kuyper. Yet, while the formal likeness of these two narratives of autonomy may be striking, could it not just be a coincidence?

First of all, it is important to note the uniqueness of the concept of freedom in Schelling's metaphysics as outlined in *Of Human Freedom*.[21] Schelling,

21. See, e.g., White (1983: 108): "Schelling begins his introduction [to *Of Human Freedom*] by asserting that the problem of freedom can be treated neither in isolation from nor as subordinate to any other philosophical issue: if freedom is worthy of philosophical treatment at all, that is, if it is real, then it must be 'one of the ruling central points of the system' (7:336). Yet, according to a common belief, there can be a philosophical system only if the world itself is a system so complete and closed as to leave no room for anything as essentially indeterminate as freedom. Schelling asserts that the problem is not insoluble: an infinite intellect would be able to account for freedom systematically. He insists also that even if human reason, in its finitude, cannot develop the absolute knowledge in which freedom and necessity are reconciled, no

"the Proteus of German Idealism," as he has been called, continued to develop and change his philosophy all throughout his career. That is not to say, of course, that there are no constants in his thought, but only to note its originality. Indeed, as White (1983: 5) notes, his philosophy can be characterized as a continual quest for a system of freedom in antithesis to Spinoza's *Ethics*. In *Of Human Freedom*, he makes room for real freedom — as opposed to the merely ideal freedom of Kant and Fichte — where the antithesis of good and evil is not resolved by synthesis (e.g., Hegel) but rather by the suppression of evil and the free fulfillment of good in love. This open, dynamic, and proto-existentialist system sets Schelling apart from his contemporaries, in part beginning with the influence of Jacob Böhme on his thought in *Of Human Freedom*.[22] While

argument will ever overcome the philosophical desire for such knowledge (7:337)." In his later thought, Schelling would continue to differentiate himself from Hegel through the concept of freedom. As Bowie (1994: 27) writes, "In his system [in his *Initia Philosophiae Universae*], Schelling, like Hegel, wishes to avoid Spinozism, and he therefore seems to follow Hegel's doctrine that the 'substance is subject,' by insisting that what is in question as the condition of possibility of the system is the 'absolute subject,' the condition of all predicates. The absolute subject cannot be characterized by a predicate, as that would contradict its essence: 'this One subject must go through everything and remain in nothing. For if it remained anywhere, life and development would be hindered. *To go through everything and to be nothing,* namely not to *be* anything such that it could not also be otherwise — this is the demand' (*Initia*, pp. 16-17). The crucial factor is the subject's ability to 'enclose itself in a form and not to do so,' its 'freedom': this is evidently a development of a central aspect of the *Ages of the World*. By talking of freedom in this way, one would seem to characterise the subject by the predicate. However, the freedom of the subject is not a determinable attribute, because, as we just saw, the subject can be *both* A and not-A, enclosed in a form and not enclosed. This point is fundamental. Freedom in this view is the ground of the world's being disclosed in ways which we cannot attribute to the activity of our consciousness. *What* we know is, as in Spinoza, determined in reflexive terms; the fact *that* we know cannot be."

22. For example, Hayner (1967: 168) notes that "beginning with *Of Human Freedom*, Schelling's investigations were strongly influenced by the writings of the theosophist, Jacob Böhme. Particularly, it seems, it was Böhme's conception of the theogonic process which captured Schelling's imagination. The mystic's analysis of this process into a three-fold pattern of creativity, in which God is to be viewed as the primal ground or ungrounded which achieves expression through the 'nature in God,' the will, provided Schelling, no doubt, with the fundamentals of the metaphysical scheme which he embraced in his positive philosophy." See Marx (1984: 60): "As far as an account of the various influences involved in various stages in Schelling's thought are concerned, the answer appears to be simple. Schelling began to read the works of the theosophist Friedrich Christoph Oetinger as early as 1803. Oetinger, in turn, was familiar with the writings of the Church Fathers, the mystics, and the cabbala; with Paracelsus, Emanuel Swedenborg, and the Swabian theologian Johann Albrecht Bengel; and, above all, with the theosophic mysticism of Jakob Böhme. During Schelling's stay in Munich from 1805

he is certainly influenced by his times and did not work in a vacuum, he also makes a unique contribution.

Kuyper, too, has made a unique contribution to his times, not in metaphysics but in Christian social thought, viz. his concept of sphere sovereignty. The question I pose is whether the narrative of autonomy in Schelling's metaphysics can be termed an influence on Kuyper's narrative of autonomy in his sphere sovereignty. Since Kuyper does not directly cite Schelling in this context, which is what is needed for conclusive proof, I argue rather that the echo of Schelling can be heard in Kuyper.

In his early years, as I have already mentioned, Kuyper not only encountered but embraced modernist lines of thought inspired by German idealism, including F. W. J. Schelling, through the channel of Scholten, as well as, I will add, Kuenen and Rauwenhoff at Leiden. As Heslam (1998: 30-31) summarizes it, "According to his own admission . . . Kuyper had lost the faith he had professed as a child, and had become intellectually and emotionally enthralled with the theology of the Leiden School." His soul was not bound to it forever though, and by a profound conversion he would later embrace and champion the more traditional Calvinism for which he is known.

If Kuyper had no knowledge of Schelling, then coincidence, rather than influence, would be the most logical conclusion. However, Kuyper not only was aware of Schelling but "drank the water," so to speak, of German idealism for a significant period early in his life.[23] Indeed, the German academy influenced all education in Europe at that time, as Kuyper (1898: 13) himself observed:

> In France since the second Napoleon came forward, we find only middling sized capacities; while in Germany a host of heroes and genii arose, and German thought, German science, German education ruled all Europe and took the lead in every department of science. . . . In twenty-five years Germany worked itself up to the full measure of its grandeur, and then already it could have been prophecied [sic] that henceforward the combined spirit of the German philosophical, historical and artistic school should put its stamp upon the next period of our human culture.[24]

until 1806, he became acquainted with Böhme's teachings in particular, as well as with those of St. Martin, Johannes Tauler, Meister Eckhart, and Nicolaus Cues through Franz von Baader."

23. According to Heslam (1999: 21n39), Kuyper himself categorizes Schelling among the idealists with regards to aesthetics.

24. Significantly, in this same work Kuyper (1898: 12) speaks of "the new *German philosophy,* from Kant to Schelling, which in its splendid enthusiasm for organic oneness and

Furthermore, in the form he encountered it, there is no doubt that Schelling's influence would have been "in the water," even apart from direct encounter.[25]

Now suppose, for example, that a songwriter has a period of her life when she is really "into" Fiona Apple, and then she moves on. That time in her life was her "Fiona Apple period," but she is "over it" now. However, suppose she then writes a song that bears a striking resemblance to "Shadowboxer" by Fiona Apple. Sure, the lyrics and instrumentation are different, but the chord progression and melody are almost the same. We do not call such similarity a coincidence; rather, we call it an influence.

Kuyper's narrative of autonomy in his concept of sphere sovereignty bears a striking resemblance to Schelling's narrative in his metaphysics in *Of Human Freedom*. Whether this influence is direct or mediated — perhaps through von Hartmann or Scholten — is unknown, but it is there. Kuyper, like the songwriter, may have been truly "over it" with regards to modernist theology. Nevertheless, in this particular "song" the lingering influence can still be heard. Those who would wish to reject this thesis would need to demonstrate some other source, not tied to Schelling, from which Kuyper's narrative springs. Absent that, the case for Schelling's influence is strong.

To be clear, however, I am not arguing that Kuyper is necessarily duplicitous or confused or conflicted, but rather simply that one seed of his earlier period, in this case, bore positive fruit in his more mature work, perhaps showing an openness, whether consciously or not, to yet find and appropriate something good from the liberal academy of his day. After all, he would not have denied the working of common grace there, even while adamantly declaiming the antithesis that too often reared its head.

REFERENCE LIST

Bowie, A. 1994. "Translator's Introduction." In F. W. J. Schelling, *On the History of Modern Philosophy*, trans. A. Bowie, pp. 1-37. Cambridge: Cambridge University Press.

Bratt, J. D. 2013. *Abraham Kuyper: Modern Calvinist, Christian Democrat.* Grand Rapids: Eerdmans.

Chiereghin, F. 2009. "Freedom and Thought: Stoicism, Skepticism, and Unhappy

systematical conception, felt painfully offended by the disintegration to which the French revolution had submitted our entire life and thought."

25. For a brief, general account of Schelling's influence, see White 1983: 1-4.

Consciousness." In *The Blackwell Guide to Hegel's Phenomenology of Spirit,* ed. K. R. Westphal, pp. 55-71. Malden, MA, and Oxford: Wiley-Blackwell.

Cooper, J. W. 2006. *Panentheism: The Other God of the Philosophers.* Grand Rapids: Baker Academic.

Eglinton, J. 2010. "Bavinck's Organic Motif: Questions Seeking Answers." *Calvin Theological Journal* 45 (April): 51-71.

———. 2012. *Trinity and Organism: Toward a New Reading of Bavinck's Organic Motif.* T&T Clark Studies in Systematic Theology 17. London and New York: T&T Clark.

Fackenheim, E. L. 1996. *The God Within: Kant, Schelling, and Historicity.* Toronto: University of Toronto Press.

Findlay, J. N. 1977. "Analysis." In G. W. F. Hegel, *Phenomenology of Spirit,* trans. A. V. Miller. Oxford: Clarendon Press.

Forster, M. 1993. "Hegel's Dialectical Method." In *The Cambridge Companion to Hegel,* ed. F. C. Beiser, pp. 130-70. Cambridge: Cambridge University Press.

Gardner, S. 2010. "Eduard von Hartmann's *Philosophy of the Unconscious.*" In *Thinking the Unconscious: Nineteenth Century German Thought,* ed. A. Nicholls and M. Liebscher. Cambridge: Cambridge University Press.

Hayner, P. C. 1967. *Reason and Existence: Schelling's Philosophy of History.* Leiden: Brill.

Hegel, G. W. F. 1977. *Phenomenology of Spirit,* trans. A. V. Miller. Oxford: Clarendon Press.

Heidegger, M. 1985. *Schelling's Treatise on the Essence of Human Freedom,* trans. J. Stambaugh. Athens, OH: Ohio University Press.

Heslam, P. S. 1998. *Creating a Christian Worldview: Abraham Kuyper's Lectures on Calvinism.* Grand Rapids: Eerdmans.

———. 1999. "A Theology of the Arts: Kuyper's Ideas on Art and Religion." In *Kuyper Reconsidered: Aspects of His Life and Work,* ed. C. van der Kooi and J. de Bruijn, pp. 13-29. VU Studies on Protestant History 3. Amsterdam: VU Uitgeverij.

Kuyper, A. 1893. "Pantheism's Destruction of Boundaries — Part I," trans. J. Hendrik de Vries. *Methodist Review* 75, no. 4: 520-34.

———. 1898. *The Antithesis Between Symbolism and Revelation: Lecture Delivered Before the Historical Presbyterian Society in Philadelphia, PA.* Edinburgh: T&T Clark.

———. 1931. *Lectures on Calvinism.* Grand Rapids: Eerdmans.

———. 1998. "Sphere Sovereignty." In *Abraham Kuyper: A Centennial Reader,* ed. J. D. Bratt, pp. 461-90. Grand Rapids: Eerdmans.

———. 2011. *Wisdom & Wonder: Common Grace in Science & Art.* Grand Rapids: Christian's Library Press.

———. 2013. *Rooted & Grounded,* trans. N. D. Kloosterman. Grand Rapids: Christian's Library Press.

Marx, W. 1984. "The Task of Schelling's *Philosophical Inquiries into the Essence of Hu-*

man Freedom." In W. Marx, *The Philosophy of F. W. J. Schelling,* trans. T. Nenon, pp. 58-85. Bloomington: Indiana University Press.

Mattson, B. 2012. *Restored to Our Destiny: Eschatology & the Image of God in Herman Bavinck's Reformed Dogmatics.* Leiden and Boston: Brill.

Neuhouser, F. 2009. "Desire, Recognition, and the Relation between Bondsman and Lord." In *The Blackwell Guide to Hegel's Phenomenology of Spirit,* ed. K. R. Westphal, pp. 37-54. Malden, MA, and Oxford: Wiley-Blackwell.

Schelling, F. W. J. 1936. *Of Human Freedom,* trans. J. Gutmann. Chicago: The Open Court Publishing Company.

———. 1966. *On University Studies,* trans. E. S. Morgan. Athens, OH: Ohio University Press.

———. 1989. *The Philosophy of Art,* ed. and trans. D. W. Stott. Minneapolis: University of Minnesota Press.

von Hartmann, E. 1931. *Philosophy of the Unconscious,* new edition in one volume, trans. W. C. Coupland. London: Routledge & Kegan Paul.

White, A. 1983. *Schelling: An Introduction to the System of Freedom.* New Haven and London: Yale University Press.

Wirth, J. M. 2005. "Animalization: Schelling and the Problem of Expressivity." In *Schelling Now: Contemporary Readings,* ed. J. M. Wirth, pp. 84-100. Bloomington: Indiana University Press.

Young, W. 1952. *Toward a Reformed Philosophy.* Grand Rapids: Piet Hein Publishers.

The Pulpit, the Lectern, and the Sickbed: Comparing Dietrich Bonhoeffer and Herman Bavinck on Church and Academy

Javier A. Garcia

Introduction

This article focuses upon two theologians who, for the pressing reasons of their distinct historical contexts, immersed themselves in both church and academy, while carefully considering the limits and negotiations between them: Dietrich Bonhoeffer (1906-1945) and Herman Bavinck (1854-1921). It examines the period when the issue of the relationship between church and academy was particularly acute for these respective thinkers. For Bonhoeffer, this was the time of great personal development and national upheaval during the years 1931 to 1933, and for Bavinck it revolved around the epoch-defining 1876 Law Concerning Higher Education. This paper contributes to the relatively new and unchartered scholarly territory of comparing Bonhoeffer and neo-Calvinism.[1] Moreover, the final aim of this study is to propose how this conversation between Bonhoeffer and Bavinck can respond to current challenges in relating these two institutions. If Bavinck and Bonhoeffer, who when taken together coincided with the major changes in academic theology's self-understanding from the late nineteenth century to the mid-twentieth century, were able to reconcile these two spheres, how might we learn from them today?

1. For previous work on Bonhoeffer and neo-Calvinism, see the following: Harinck and Dekker 2007: 86-98. Besides this study, Bonhoeffer and neo-Calvinism have been mentioned side by side, but without much comparative analysis: Huntemann 1989: 88-89; De Gruchy 1984: 105ff. For a more recent comparison, see Himes 2012. I would like to thank Brant Himes for drawing my attention to these references.

To this end, this study consists of three parts: convergences, divergences, and contemporary suggestions.

In what remains of the introduction, a word should be said about Bonhoeffer's and Bavinck's ecclesial and academic involvement.

Bonhoeffer's life was especially enmeshed in these two worlds. After an inspiring trip to Rome when he was 18, Bonhoeffer dedicated his doctoral dissertation *Sanctorum Communio* to ecclesiology. His theological formation at the University of Berlin by such eminent figures as Karl Holl, Adolf von Harnack, Reinhold Seeberg, and, from afar, Karl Barth, gave him a lifelong appreciation for the importance of academic theology. Following a year as pastor to an expat German congregation in Barcelona and a postdoctoral fellowship at New York's Union Seminary, Bonhoeffer plunged into various ecclesial and academic activities in Berlin from 1931 to 1933. He is perhaps best known for his contribution to the Confessing Church during the *Kirchenkampf*, including his time as the director of the illegal seminary, Finkenwalde, from 1935 to 1937. There he penned his most famous and deeply ecclesiological texts *Discipleship* and *Life Together.* Although his right to teach at the university was revoked in August 1936 and his role in the German resistance against Hitler after 1940 meant less direct pastoral or teaching responsibilities, Bonhoeffer continued to engage ecclesiology and academic theology in what would posthumously become his *Ethics* and *Letters and Papers from Prison.* It is no exaggeration, then, to say that Bonhoeffer was active in both contexts, whether directly or indirectly, throughout his life.

The same can be said of Bavinck. Like Bonhoeffer, Bavinck's theological formation would have a lasting influence on his perception of academic theology. Rather than staying at the theological seminary of his Christian Reformed Church in Kampen, where he studied from 1873 to 1874, Bavinck controversially decided to receive his education at the University of Leiden, whose theology faculty was "renowned for its aggressively modernist, 'scientific' approach to theology" (Bolt 2003: 13).[2] After graduating from Leiden in 1880, and a brief pastorate in the small town of Franeker from 1881 to 1882, Bavinck joined the faculty at Kampen in 1883, where he taught for just under two decades. In 1902, Bavinck became Professor of Theology at the Free University of Amsterdam, where he remained until the end of his career. It would

2. Although some scholars have suggested this resulted in an enduring tension in Bavinck's works between modernism and Reformed orthodoxy as well as between worldliness or a pietistic separation from culture, others have more convincingly argued against this "two Bavincks" thesis in favor of a unified reading of his thought. See Eglinton 2012.

be a mistake, however, to caricature Bavinck as an ivory tower theologian given this primarily academic path. Along with Abraham Kuyper, Bavinck was heavily involved in the considerable ecclesiastical shifts in the Netherlands in the late nineteenth century, which resulted in the formation of the *Gereformeerde Kerken in Nederland* in 1892 (Eglinton 2012: 23-24). Moreover, Bavinck recognized the dangers in ecclesiology developing in the Dutch academic theology circles of his time, such as in the Groninger and Leiden schools, and reworked his Reformed tradition to oppose them (Eglinton 2012: 6-18). Bavinck's theological efforts, including his magnum opus, *Reformed Dogmatics,* cannot be understood apart from this ecclesial concern.

Similarities and Convergences

As a point of basic biographical convergence, Bonhoeffer and Bavinck were faced with historical situations that demanded a clear formulation of the relationship between church and academy.

Bonhoeffer's biographer Eberhard Bethge relates that "Bonhoeffer decided to be a minister and theologian when he was a boy, and he never seems to have wavered in this ambition" (Bethge 2000: 36). The period 1931-33 marks the height of Bonhoeffer's dual career path in the ministry and the academy. In reality, Bonhoeffer found himself overwhelmed by the competing demands of three realms of work, which nevertheless remained within the purview of these interests: the University of Berlin where he lectured, the Zionskirche where he was assistant pastor, and the international ecumenical movement in which he served as youth secretary of the World Alliance for Promoting International Friendship among the Churches. Moreover, aggressive Nazi interference drove Bonhoeffer to reconceive the relation between church and academy. On the one hand, the nationalist German Christian movement, which would spark the Church Struggle, was founded in May 1932 (Lukens, Barnett, and Brocker 2012: 2). On the other, Günther Dehn, a pastor and socialist, was dismissed from his theology professorship in Halle in 1932 and blocked from a professorship in Heidelberg for his pacifist views, due to National Socialist opposition. The highly publicized "Dehn Affair" was the first occasion on which Bonhoeffer publicly opposed the growing national right wing from his own initiative (Strohm 2012: 482). For these reasons, he makes some of his clearest statements on the church and academy during this period.

Bavinck faced a different challenge in his time, which nevertheless produced the same urgency to define the relation between these institutions. John

Bolt provides the background to Bavinck's first volume of his *Reformed Dogmatics* when he writes:

> the ecclesiastical and academic context in which these questions lived and moved and had their being was the 1876 Law Concerning Higher Education, which effectively turned university theology into departments of religious studies. Rather than a confessionally normative dogmatic theology, a neutral, phenomenological approach to religion was mandated by law. (Bolt 2003: 19)

It is important to keep in mind the historical context leading up to this law. In the mid-nineteenth century, higher education in the Netherlands was caught between two approaches: the German *Bildung* model and pre-vocational education. The dominant view at the beginning of the century was expressed in the *Organiek Besluit* decree of 1815, which "stated that the task of the universities was to prepare young noblemen for a life in the highest circles" (Bank and van Buuren 2004: 245). It effectively promoted divisions between the aristocracy and the middle class by marking a stark difference between university education and professional practice. In response, the Ewijck government, led by the minister for home affairs, Johan Rudolf Thorbecke, pushed towards a pre-vocational model, which would incorporate the needs of professional practice into higher education and break down this class divide. The Secondary Education Act of 1863 implemented this radical shift in educational policy. Interestingly, however, Thorbecke was also influenced by the key concept of *Bildung* in the German system. Following Wilhem von Humboldt's lead, Thorbecke believed education should instill "civilization" through "knowledge *(Wissenschaft)* of the classics" (Bank and van Buuren 2004: 246). Crucially, the German example of *Bildung durch Wissenschaft* contained many similarities to the "learning" described in *Organiek Besluit.* As a result, the Higher Education Act of 1876 reflected Thorbecke's mixed influences:

> On the one hand it created some scope for pre-vocational university education, but on the other it made it clear that this was a secondary but not strictly proper aim for a university, whose first and foremost task was to civilize the youth of the elite. (Bank and van Buuren 2004: 246)

This engendered a crisis over the place of theology in the university: would it belong to the practical subjects of pre-vocational training, or to the academic subjects as part of the *Bildung* side of education, or should it be eliminated altogether? In his essay "Theology and Religious Studies," Bavinck laments the consequence of these debates when he states,

> After numerous fits and starts, proposals and counterproposals, and much parliamentary maneuvering, the 1876 Law of Higher Education created a curious anomaly: The *name* of the faculties of *theology* was retained, but the *content* of what was to be taught effectively made them departments of religious studies. *In this way theology was maimed and robbed of its heart and life.* (Bavinck 2008: 53; emphasis original)

Bavinck's decision as a young man to study in Leiden, as well as his later move from Kampen to the Free University of Amsterdam, reflects his "ideal of a scientific theology," which "required a university setting" (Bolt 2003: 19). The *Prolegomena* to *Reformed Dogmatics* contains Bavinck's defense of dogmatic theology as a science that belongs side by side with other sciences in the university, against its replacement by religious studies.

From the outset, Bonhoeffer and Bavinck agree on the intrinsic interrelation between church and academy. The fundamental link that ties these two together for both theologians is the word of God in Holy Scripture.

Bonhoeffer argues that the task of the church is to discern God's concrete commandment in the word of God. In a letter to his friend Erwin Sutz from 1932, Bonhoeffer articulates the primary challenge of ethics and preaching in sacramental terms. He states, "Basically, it all depends on the problem of ethics, that is, actually on the question of whether it is possible for the concrete commandment to be proclaimed through the church." He gets to the heart of the problem when he continues, "The concrete form of the proclamation of grace is, after all, the sacrament. But what is the sacrament of the ethical, of the commandment?" (Bonhoeffer 2012e: 136-37). Otherwise stated, if the sacrament concretizes the gospel by lending physicality to the promise, how can the attendant commandment be rendered equally concrete?

In order to understand how Bonhoeffer resolves this dilemma, we must turn to his 1932 lecture delivered at the ecumenical youth conference in the then Czechoslovakia. In this text it becomes apparent that the issue of concretion touches not only on preaching, but also on the importance of theology and the identity of the church more generally. To begin, Bonhoeffer simply assumes that the World Alliance *is* the Christian church endowed with the task of speaking the word of Jesus Christ "to the entire world" (Bonhoeffer 2012a: 358-59). Reaching the question of the concrete commandment, Bonhoeffer writes somewhat cryptically, "What the sacrament is for the proclamation of the gospel, the knowledge of concrete reality is for the proclamation of the commandment. *Reality is the sacrament of the commandment*" (Bonhoeffer 2012a: 361).[3] The descriptive task of preaching must stem from a deep knowledge of reality as rooted in creation and must speak the concrete commandment into it. But how does the church actually discern God's commandment "for this hour"? Bonhoeffer replies, "*The commandment cannot come from anywhere else except that place where the promise and fulfillment come from, namely, from Christ*" (Bonhoeffer 2012a: 362-63). Christ is so present to the church that the church must gain its knowledge of the concrete commandment from him directly. It is only from this premise that the Sermon on the Mount and the orders of preservation in creation can be interpreted correctly (Bonhoeffer 2012a: 363-64).

Likewise, academic theology depends on the word of God. For his first lecture course in the University of Berlin during the winter semester of 1931-32, Bonhoeffer chose the topic "The History of Twentieth-Century Systematic Theology." Although at first glance these lectures seem to be an introductory survey of modern theology, they "[reflect] Bonhoeffer's . . . foundational reorientation, his major 'turn' *(Wende)*, on the basis of the theology of Karl Barth" (Luckens, Barnett, and Brocker 2012: 19). The fulcrum for this turn is the centrality of the word of God for theology. According to Bonhoeffer, the decisive difference between Barth and his predecessors is that his message comes "from a new reading of the Bible . . . from God's own word spoken in God's revelation" (Bonhoeffer 2012b: 226).[4] God's word is not limited to the church, but governs all theology. With Barth, Bonhoeffer affirms "*Deus dixit* — to accept this is the beginning of all genuine theological thinking" (Bonhoeffer 2012b: 231). Thus the word of God is determinative for both spheres, church and academy, since they both seek a theology of the word of God. Despite his appreciation of his mentor's contribution to systematic theology, Bonhoeffer critiques Barth for understanding ethics as demonstration, since this "excludes any concrete teaching" (Bonhoeffer 2012b: 244). Barth changed everything in

3. (All italics cited are original to the text). While a full explanation of these statements would require an excursus into Bonhoeffer's doctrine of creation and his use of Luther's early sacramentology, it suffices to say for our purposes that "the (ethical) word spoken by the Church as God's command is validated by knowledge of the reality of the fallen world 'only insofar as this reality is itself wholly grounded in its relationship to the reality of creation'" (Plant 2005: 81).

4. It is important to note here that, "Although the *Deus dixit* axiom is closely associated with the writings of Karl Barth, it should be acknowledged that Barth borrowed this emphasis from Bavinck" (Eglinton and Bräutigam 2013: 47). See Bavinck 1928: 22; Barth 1982: 65.

signaling the supremacy of the word of God, but lost its power in the crucial point of concretion. Bonhoeffer's conclusion to these lectures encapsulates his diagnosis of the church and academy during this period. He remarks,

> Our messages from the church have so little power because they sit in the middle, between general principles and concrete situations. The trouble with the church [is] also the trouble with theological faculties, but this trouble is so little noticed.
>
> Luther was able to write *On the Bondage of the Will* and his piece on usury at the same time. Why can't we do that anymore? (Bonhoeffer 2012b: 244)

For Bonhoeffer, the church and academy share the same basic responsibility: concretizing the word of God, that is, applying it to present historical reality. These institutions must learn from Luther, who could explain complex theological issues on the one hand and address specific historical needs on the other. To "sit in the middle" is to forfeit the power and purpose of church and academy.

Bavinck, like Bonhoeffer, returns to the importance of Scripture in his defense of dogmatics as a science. According to Bavinck, "religious studies" carries a whole host of assumptions based on its historical development. Tracing its origins from Kant to Schleiermacher to Ritschl, Bavinck explains that, in the modern conception of religion embodied in the Higher Education Act of 1876, it is only by abandoning personal confessional allegiances and the prejudice of prizing Christianity above other religions in favor of objective investigation that dogmatics can be considered a science in the true sense of the word (Bavinck 2003: 36). The "essence of religion" replaces Scripture, confession, Christian piety, and the faith of the church as the content of dogma (Bavinck 2003: 36). Such an approach views the content of religion as immaterial, since it is solely interested in the forms of religion (Bavinck 2003: 72). This historical-comparative and experimental-psychological method finally "culminates in a philosophy of religion, a philosophical dogmatics" (Bavinck 2003: 72).

Bavinck objects to this framework from all sides in his recasting of dogmatics. Rather than a universal science, theology is a particular science; in place of vague references to an unknown generic God, theology concerns itself with the dogma of the knowable God who has revealed himself (Bavinck 2003: 38). More specifically, this revelation can be found in Scripture, the church, and the Christian consciousness, which in conjunction with one another constitute the sources for dogmatics (Bavinck 2003: 78). Bavinck embraced the final authority of *Deus dixit* before Barth and Bonhoeffer (Bavinck 2003: 30).[5] Along these lines, Bavinck debunks the essence of religion as the content of dogmatics. Without adding to it, dogmatics simply orders or "rationally reproduce[s] the content of revelation that relates to the knowledge of God" (Bavinck 2003: 45). This means that "the sole aim of dogmatics is to set forth the thoughts of God that he has laid down in Holy Scripture," not in a reductionistic so-called "Biblical Theology," but in appropriate scholarly form (Bavinck 2003: 60). Bavinck's convergence with Bonhoeffer is evidenced, then, in his prioritization of Scripture for his defense of dogmatics as a science in the university.

Furthermore, Bavinck is of one mind with Bonhoeffer regarding the ecclesial character of the academy. For Bavinck, dogmatics is an ecclesial activity that serves the church. The fact that dogmaticians operate on the principle of faith for their knowledge of God in revelation means that they are "organically connected with the church of all believers" (Bavinck 2003: 46). Instead of acting as lone scientists, dogmaticians situate themselves within a particular Christian tradition (Bavinck 2003: 82) and "[set] forth the knowledge of God that is laid down in his Word *to the church*" (Bavinck 2003: 46). Bavinck elaborates on the church-academy relation in discussing faith and theology. As he states, "Faith preserves theology from secularization; theology preserves faith from separatism. For that reason the church and the school . . . though two entities, ought to be in solidarity with each other" (Bavinck 2003: 616). This mutuality is so important that Bavinck regards the "distorted" relation between the church and theology of his day as "disastrous" (Bavinck 2003: 616).

Still, Bonhoeffer and Bavinck maintain that the specific task of academic theology is distinct to that of preaching in the church. The key distinction for Bonhoeffer here is the *actus directus* and *actus reflexus* outlined in *Act and Being*. *Actus directus* refers to direct consciousness, an unthinking knowing or intentionality, while *actus reflexus* denotes a consciousness of reflection, which displaces intentionality (Bonhoeffer 1996: 28). To simplify this jargon, these terms can be situated in the context of faith. The former describes the objective fact of faith in the believer, an immediate *fides directa,* the state of being in Christ, whereas the latter encompasses all reflection on this fact, as a

5. "Among Reformed theologians, therefore, the following proposition returns again and again: 'the principle into which all theological dogmas are distilled is: God has said it' " (Bavinck 2003: 30). The English translation substitutes "God has said it" for Bavinck's use of the Latin phrase *Deus dixit*. See note 4 above.

how for the *that* of belief. With these starting premises, Bonhoeffer delineates three ways of knowing in the church: believing, preaching, and theological. The first is simply "to know oneself overcome and pardoned by the person of Christ in the preached word" (Bonhoeffer 1996: 126). In this existential way of knowing, faith is a God-given reality whose origin cannot be questioned or scrutinized; that is, "faith rests in itself as *actus directus*" (Bonhoeffer 1996: 128). Preachers, conversely, "must know 'what' they preach," that is to say Christ; they "must reflect on the 'what' about which they preach . . . and bring it to expression" (Bonhoeffer 1996: 129). The question of theology naturally arises here, because it is required to keep preaching faithful in its task. The role of theology as a scholarly discipline is to understand the presuppositions and history of Christian preaching in order to form dogmas that can inform that preaching (Bonhoeffer 1996: 130). Essentially, theology *reflects* on the *reflection* of preaching to serve the church (Bonhoeffer 1996: 131). While preaching and theology differ for Bonhoeffer, they remain indivisible facets of the one church.

Accordingly, in his letter to the Department of Theology in Halle opposing their dismissal of Günther Dehn, Bonhoeffer forcefully argues that theologians and theological faculties are no less accountable to God in their handling of Scripture than leaders in the church; Bonhoeffer instead calls them teachers and representatives of the church (Bonhoeffer 2012d: 99-100). To emphasize the degree of responsibility in these spheres, Bonhoeffer agrees with Otto Dibelius's solution to the huge influx of theology students in the Berlin faculty, that they should be willing to accept martyrdom (Bonhoeffer 2012c: 77-78), an exigency Bonhoeffer began to place on the church as early as his days in Barcelona (Bonhoeffer 2008a: 557-58). The academy is therefore not an optional supplement but rather an integral player alongside the church in concretizing the word of God and reflecting upon it. To speak about the word of God in either context is such a weighty task that those who undertake it should be willing to accept martyrdom as a matter of principle.

Bavinck embraces a similar distinction and complementarity between theology and preaching, albeit with less intensity. Bavinck employs his distinction of the church as organism and institution to establish that theology "is not a product of the church as institution; it does not have its origin in the official ministry Christ has given his church" (Bavinck 2003: 609). Nevertheless, theology still "arises in the church of Christ" and treats the church as organism as its subject (Bavinck 2003: 609). Faith and theology remain distinct. Faith is assent to revealed truths while theology is the knowledge of them. As such, faith is the *that* to which theology is the *why* and the *how* (Bavinck

2003: 615). Yet, Bavinck adds, "they cannot do without each other" (Bavinck 2003: 616). Here Bavinck's complementary definition of faith and theology is practically identical to Bonhoeffer's description of preaching and theological knowing. More importantly, although theology does not technically belong to the church as institution, it still plays a pivotal role as a part of the larger church as organism.

Lastly, Bonhoeffer's principle of concretion finds its correlate in Bavinck's demand for the practicality of theology. For Bavinck, the right of theology to be called a science depends on its practical application to real life. As he notes in *The Certainty of Faith* from 1901,

> A theology must demonstrate its right and truth, not only in the area of science, but also and more powerfully amidst the awful realities of life — at the sickbed and deathbed, in suffering and want, in distress and death, to the guilt-laden conscience and to the heart thirsting for reconciliation and peace. If theology stands powerless in the face of these situations and is unable to provide any consolation, then it is unworthy of its place among the sciences. (Bavinck 1980: 17)

Theology must reach beyond the classroom to the real needs of the world, including those of the congregation. In demanding such concretion and protecting against esoteric uselessness, Bavinck lends greater dignity not just to theology, but to all scientific endeavors.

To summarize, Bonhoeffer and Bavinck identify Scripture as the fundamental link between church and academy, see academic theology as ecclesially grounded and directed, maintain the different roles of these institutions, and insist upon the practical application of theological inquiry to concrete reality. It is important to flesh out the radical boldness of these claims. One potential downfall that dogged the academy in Bonhoeffer and Bavinck's times was that it would descend into an objective detached institution which would be unable to respond to the grave needs of the church and the world around it. Recognizing the impossibility of neutrality, these theologians pointed to Scripture above all as the normative text for academic theology. They added yet another level of accountability and responsibility by tying the academy inextricably to the church. Although these have distinct roles to play, they are complementary and mutually beneficial, working towards the same task of faithfully interpreting Scripture in a way that has practical use in everyday life. In this way, these theologians set a compelling precedent to our understanding of the church and the academy today.

Divergences

On one level, the divergences between Bonhoeffer and Bavinck on this issue come down to a superficial difference of context, language, and emphasis. The provenance of Bavinck's preoccupation with dogmatics as a science stems from the debates of his time concerning the role of theology in the university. This places the emphasis squarely upon the proper definition of dogmatics in relation to other sciences. Bavinck's focus therefore lies with the academy, due to the historical debates that shaped his *Prolegomena.* His concern about the church comes secondarily as a derivative of this main concern. For Bonhoeffer, who rarely uses the language of dogmatics or science, the ethical commandment proclaimed by the church instead claims his attention. Nazi threats to the integrity of the academy, such as in the "Dehn Affair," compelled him to situate it in relation to his primary area of interest, the church.

On another level, Bonhoeffer and Bavinck differ substantially due to the intensity of their statements. Bonhoeffer unequivocally equates God's word with the word of the church, with the caveat that the church relies on the forgiveness of sins in making ethical pronouncements (Bonhoeffer 2012a: 361). From the beginning of his career, Bonhoeffer endorsed a risky identification of Christ and the church through his famous phrase *Christ existing as church community* (Bonhoeffer 1998: 121), which effectively made the commandments of the church (that is, those communities he considered worthy of the name) irrefutable. Some have found fault with this identification and its consequences (Huber 1980: 129-30; Bayer 1992: 249). Bonhoeffer's approach culminated when he evoked *extra ecclesiam nulla salus* against those outside the Confessing Church at the height of the Church Struggle (Barnett 2005: 7). Given the extreme nature of the demands placed upon the church in 1932 Germany, one can understand why Bonhoeffer embraces such a doctrinaire ecclesiology. Bavinck, on the other hand, thoroughly protects himself against this identification. He writes, resting his case, "The dogma that the church confesses and the dogmatician develops is not identical with the absolute truth of God itself" (Bavinck 2003: 32). Although Bonhoeffer and Bavinck seek the truth of Scripture in church and academy, Bavinck more readily accepts a critical distance between their decisions and God's council than Bonhoeffer.

In addition, the confessional divide between these theologians should be mentioned. Recent scholarship has brought to light the Lutheran provenance of Bonhoeffer's theology (DeJonge 2012: 83-97). According to this reading, while Bonhoeffer variously interacted with Reformed theology through Karl

Barth, he proposed his own Lutheran alternative. Conversely, Bavinck displays vast knowledge of other traditions, including Lutheranism, and sides decisively with the Reformed. In Bavinck's words, "the Reformed Christian thinks theologically, the Lutheran anthropologically," a difference that runs like a red line through their dogmatics (Bavinck 2003: 177). Although a thorough examination into the consequences of these confessional directions for the question of church and academy is not possible here, this difference most certainly affects their treatment of the subject.

Finally, perhaps the most telling factor separating these theologians is the divergence of their trajectories over time. While Bonhoeffer became disillusioned with the university and came to prioritize his involvement in the church, Bavinck's quest to revitalize scientific theology steered him more and more towards the academy.

As previously mentioned, 1931-32 marked the height of the young German theologian's dual career path. Upon closer examination, however, this joint endeavor ended shortly thereafter, a fact which only confirmed Bonhoeffer's persistent inclinations towards the church over the academy. According to Bethge, soon after the completion of his dissertation in 1927, Bonhoeffer's "problem was not how to enter the academic world, it was how to escape it. The pulpit appealed to him more than the professor's lectern" (Bethge 2000: 96). Further, in a letter from 1930, Bonhoeffer relates to a close friend, "I feel in general that academic work will not hold me for long. But I do acknowledge that it is quite important to acquire beforehand the best academic training possible" (Bonhoeffer 2008b: 205). Most strikingly, Bonhoeffer could say to Erwin Sutz in 1934, "I no longer believe in the university; in fact I never really believed in it" (Bonhoeffer 2007: 217). Larry Rasmussen provides a helpful analysis of this sudden change. Although, given the academic pedigree of his family, Bonhoeffer "breathed this heady air easily," the enthusiastic endorsement of fascism by prominent German intellectuals, including eminent theologians such as Paul Althaus, Gerhard Kittel, and Friedrich Gogarten, suffocated the young lecturer's hopes for the university (Rasmussen 2009: 4). Despite his circle of loyal students, "Bonhoeffer would soon find himself a stranger in his own profession," as he "began to question the allegiances he had taken for granted and the career he had assumed" (Rasmussen 2009: 4-5). Rasmussen summarizes this sudden disabuse of earlier ambitions when he writes, "In short, Bonhoeffer had decided that 'credible Christian praxis and community was more important than his academic career' in almost the same moment he embarked on that career" (Rasmussen 2009: 5). The academy no longer seemed a viable option for hearing the call to discipleship and discerning the word of God. Instead, Bonhoeffer devoted himself entirely to the church struggle, a move which was solidified when his teaching rights at the University of Berlin were rescinded in August 1936 (Bethge 2000: 516). This turned out to be a blessing in disguise as "the period of training seminarians, from 1935 to 1939, was a time during which Bonhoeffer's many abilities came most coherently together, years in which he truly seems to have found his vocation" (Barnett 2005: 9). For Bonhoeffer, the future of the church demanded a new form of theological education that the university could not provide. As he writes, continuing his letter to Erwin Sutz in 1934,

> The next generation of pastors, these days, ought to be trained entirely in church-monastic schools, where the pure doctrine, the Sermon on the Mount, and worship are taken seriously — which for all three of these things is simply not the case at the university and under the present circumstances is impossible. (Bonhoeffer 2007: 217)

Therefore, there came a certain point when Bonhoeffer was willing to abandon the university for the calling of the church due to the prime concern of hearing the word of God during the *Kirchenkampf.*

Bavinck, burdened by the need to provide orthodox theology in the university, dedicated his energies fully to this institution. Developments in nineteenth-century Dutch theology help to account for this impulse. According to Jan Bank and Maarten van Buuren, "In the second half of the nineteenth century Protestantism in the Netherlands . . . was marked by a confrontation between so-called modern theology and orthodoxy" (2004: 311). From its beginnings in Utrecht in 1800 to its development in Groningen in 1830 and its culmination in Leiden around 1860, modern Dutch theology challenged the basic tenets of traditional Protestant doctrine (Bank and van Buuren 2004: 313-15).[6] Churches bore the brunt of these debates, as newly trained ministers disseminated modernism through the pulpit, producing a backlash of orthodoxy in many congregations (Bank and van Buuren 2004: 318-19). By the time Kuyper founded the Free University in 1890, he was recognized as the theological and political leader of the orthodox movement (Bank and van Buuren 2004: 324). The Free University was conceived as "a

6. Led by Jan Hendrik Scholten (1811-1885), this modernist movement denied supernaturalism (including miracles and the resurrection), challenged the reliability of Scripture through historical criticism, and championed human autonomy against the traditional Reformed doctrine of total depravity and redemption achieved exclusively by God.

Protestant university free of state influence," which would provide an orthodox Reformed alternative to modernist education (Bank and van Buuren 2004: 328). In the realm of theology, the new university became the setting for the systematic development of neo-Calvinism. Kuyper led the way, completing his magnum opus, *Encyclopaedie der Heilige Godgeleerdheid,* in three volumes between 1893 and 1894. This theological background, coupled with the changes in education during this time, provides the backdrop for Bavinck's firmly academic intentions. Unlike Bonhoeffer, Bavinck's main mission was to drive theology into the heart of the university, both to secure its rightful place among the sciences and to oppose the threat of modern theology. His relationship to Leiden University illustrates his lifelong passion for theology in the academy. Not only did he choose it for his studies, but he was devastated not to receive a permanent position to teach dogmatics there in 1889 (De Bruijn and Harinck 1999: 138).[7] In Kampen, Bavinck already expressed his desire to leave for Amsterdam or Leiden, citing he missed the Leiden library (De Bruijn and Harinck 1999: 131). As the bastion of modern theology, Leiden would have been the ideal place for him to counter its teachings and bolster theology among the sciences. Nevertheless, he fulfilled this hope by replacing Abraham Kuyper as Professor of Theology at the Free University of Amsterdam in 1902. Here he completed the *Reformed Dogmatics.* As Bank and van Buuren conclude, "Both Kuyper and Bavinck gave the orthodox campaign an intellectual foundation, and thus secured the same position as the Leiden theologian Scholten with his systematic theology of modernism" (2004: 329). In contrast to his short stint as a pastor in Franeker, then, Bavinck made it his enduring goal to contribute to university theology. As such, Bonhoeffer and Bavinck understood their calling and the needs of their historical moments differently, as illustrated by their concentration on church and academy respectively.

Conclusion

In conclusion, what can we learn from Bonhoeffer and Bavinck about the church and academy today? A helpful way to bridge the gap between then

7. Shortly after the death of L. W. E. Rauwenhoff, who taught dogmatics, philosophy of religion, and encyclopedia at Leiden, on 26 January 1889, Bavinck wrote to his friend Christiaan Snouck Hurgronje that, "Eerlijk beken ik, dat een leerstoel als dien Rauwenhoff innam, voor mij veel bekoorlijke heeft" (I honestly admit that a chair like the one Rauwenhoff occupied is very attractive to me) (de Bruijn and Harinck 1999: 138).

and now is to present a case study of a university which has attempted to learn from academic theology in the nineteenth and twentieth centuries for the development of its divinity faculty: the University of Cambridge. David Ford, the Regius Professor of the Divinity Faculty in Cambridge since 1991, admires the vision implemented by Schleiermacher at the University of Berlin. Against Fichte, the university's first Rector, "who wanted to exclude theology because it was not sufficiently '*wissenschaftlich*,'" his successor Schleiermacher successfully incorporated theology alongside the other disciplines with the aim of the professional education of the clergy (Ford 2007: 129). Ford commends Schleiermacher for creating a "religious and secular" university, which preserved the particularity of Christianity while still engaging the "religious nature" of Berlin society at the time (Ford 2007: 127). Effectively, this arrangement tied the church and the academy together in a manner which was beneficial to the church and society at large. In a world that is increasingly religious and secular at the same time, Ford believes both elements must be present in the university, as they were under Schleiermacher (Ford 2007: 129). Ford therefore proposes *theology and religious studies* as the model that should shape theological faculties in the future. This paradigm satisfies the particularity of each religion and their religious communities, including the church, while still contributing to the larger "ecosystem" of ideas required by the modern university (Ford 2011: 150-54). According to Ford, the main "stake holders" involved — religious communities, pluralist democracies, and universities — "all stand to gain" from this model (Ford 2011: 154).

How would the Divinity Faculty in Cambridge and other contemporary theology departments, considering their curriculum, respond to the positions taken by Bonhoeffer and Bavinck in their own times? Would there be a real tension between the unapologetic (and at times radical) boldness of faith these theologians propose and the delicate pluralism assumed in theology and religious studies? To what extent is Bavinck's statement "*theology and religious studies are incompatible and cannot be contained in one department*" true (Bavinck 2008: 54)? Can a faithful and practical reading of Holy Scripture in cooperation with the church flourish under these circumstances? Or, will Christians have no choice but to leave the academy in search of a more serious examination of the word of God? Can the academy match the seminary in its devotion to this endeavor? Taken together, Bavinck and Bonhoeffer draw our attention to the vitality of the Christian faith when it is explicated and lived out by the different interdependent parts of the one body of Christ. Yet the question remains for our time of whether and how the church and academy will succeed in cooperating for their mutual welfare.

REFERENCES

Bank, Jan, and Maarten van Buuren. 2004. *1900: The Age of Bourgeois Culture,* vol. 3 of *Dutch Culture in a European Perspective.* Assen: Royal Van Gorcum.

Barnett, Victoria. 2012. "Introduction." In *Theological Education Underground: 1937-40,* vol. 15 of *Dietrich Bonhoeffer Works,* English Edition, ed. Victoria J. Barnett, trans. Victoria J. Barnett et al. Minneapolis: Fortress Press.

Barth, Karl. 1982. "Gesamtausgabe." In *Christliche Dogmatik im Entwurf,* vol. 1, ed. Gerhard Sauter. Zurich: Theologischer Verlag.

Bavinck, Herman. 1928. *Gereformeerde Dogmatiek,* 4e druk, 1e deel. Kampen: Kok.

———. 1980. *The Certainty of Faith,* trans. H. der Nederlanden. St. Catharines: Paideia Press.

———. 2003. *Reformed Dogmatics,* vol. 1, ed. John Bolt, trans. John Vriend. Grand Rapids: Baker.

———. 2008. "Theology and Religious Studies." In *Essays on Religion, Science, and Society,* ed. John Bolt, trans. Harry Boonstra and Gerrit Sheeres. Grand Rapids: Baker Academic.

Bayer, Oswald. 1992. "Christus als Mitte: Bonhoeffers Ethik im Banne der Religionsphilosophie Hegels?" In *Leibliches Wort: Reformation und Neuzeit im Konflikt,* ed. Oswald Bayer. Tübingen: J. C. B. Mohr.

Bethge, Eberhard. 2000. *Dietrich Bonhoeffer: A Biography,* ed. Victoria J. Barnett. Revised edition. Minneapolis: Fortress Press.

Bolt, John. 2003. "Introduction." In Herman Bavinck, *Reformed Dogmatics,* vol. 1, ed. John Bolt, trans. John Vriend. Grand Rapids: Baker.

Bonhoeffer, Dietrich. 1996. *Act and Being: Transcendental Philosophy and Ontology in Systematic Theology,* vol. 2 of *Dietrich Bonhoeffer Works,* English Edition, ed. Wayne Whitson Floyd Jr., trans. H. Martin Rumscheidt. Minneapolis: Fortress Press.

———. 1998. *Sanctorum Communio: A Theological Study of the Sociology of the Church,* vol. 1 of *Dietrich Bonhoeffer Works,* English Edition, ed. Clifford J. Green, trans. Reinhard Krauss and Nancy Lukens. Minneapolis: Fortress Press.

———. 2007. "To Erwin Sutz, London, September 11, 1934." In *London: 1933-35,* vol. 13 of *Dietrich Bonhoeffer Works,* English Edition, ed. Keith Clements, trans. Isabel Best and Douglas W. Stott. Minneapolis: Fortress Press.

———. 2008a. "Homily for the Children's Service, Berlin (?), Remembrance Sunday, November 24, 1929 (?)." In *Barcelona, Berlin, New York: 1928-31,* vol. 10 of *Dietrich Bonhoeffer Works,* English Edition, ed. Clifford Green, trans. Douglas W. Stott. Minneapolis: Fortress Press.

———. 2008b. "To Helmut Rößler, Berlin, February 23, 1930." In *Barcelona, Berlin, New York: 1928-31,* vol. 10 of *Dietrich Bonhoeffer Works,* English Edition, ed. Clifford Green, trans. Douglas W. Stott. Minneapolis: Fortress Press.

———. 2012a. "Lecture in Ciernohorské Kúpele: On the Theological Foundation of the Work of the World Alliance." In *Ecumenical, Academic, and Pastoral Work: 1931-32,* vol. 11 of the *Dietrich Bonhoeffer Works,* English Edition, ed. Victoria J. Barnett, Mark S. Brocker, and Michael B. Luckens, trans. Anne Schmidt-Lange et al. Minneapolis: Fortress Press.

———. 2012b. "Lecture Course: The History of Twentieth-Century Systematic Theology (Student Notes)." In *Ecumenical, Academic, and Pastoral Work: 1931-32,* vol. 11 of the *Dietrich Bonhoeffer Works,* English Edition, ed. Victoria J. Barnett, Mark S. Brocker, and Michael B. Luckens, trans. Anne Schmidt-Lange et al. Minneapolis: Fortress Press.

———. 2012c. "To Erwin Sutz, Berlin, December 25, 1931." In *Ecumenical, Academic, and Pastoral Work: 1931-32,* vol. 11 of the *Dietrich Bonhoeffer Works,* English Edition, ed. Victoria J. Barnett, Mark S. Brocker, and Michael B. Luckens, trans. Anne Schmidt-Lange et al. Minneapolis: Fortress Press.

———. 2012d. "Draft Submission to the Department of Theology in Halle concerning the Dehn Case, March 1932." In *Ecumenical, Academic, and Pastoral Work: 1931-32,* vol. 11 of the *Dietrich Bonhoeffer Works,* English Edition, ed. Victoria J. Barnett, Mark S. Brocker, and Michael B. Luckens, trans. Anne Schmidt-Lange et al. Minneapolis: Fortress Press.

———. 2012e. "To Erwin Sutz, Berlin, August 1932." In *Ecumenical, Academic, and Pastoral Work: 1931-32,* vol. 11 of the *Dietrich Bonhoeffer Works,* English Edition, ed. Victoria J. Barnett, Mark S. Brocker, and Michael B. Luckens, trans. Anne Schmidt-Lange et al. Minneapolis: Fortress Press.

De Bruijn, Jan, and George Harinck. 1999. *Een Leidse Vriendschap.* Baarn: Ten Have.

De Gruchy, John. 1984. *Bonhoeffer and South Africa: Theology in Dialogue.* Grand Rapids: Eerdmans.

DeJonge, Michael. 2012. *Bonhoeffer's Theological Formation: Berlin, Barth, and Protestant Theology.* Oxford: Oxford University Press.

Eglinton, James. 2012. *Trinity and Organism: Towards a New Reading of Herman Bavinck's Organic Motif.* London: T&T Clark.

Eglinton, James, and Michael Bräutigam. 2013. "Scientific Theology? Herman Bavinck and Adolf Schlatter on the Place of Theology in the University." *Journal of Reformed Theology* 7: 27-50.

Ford, David F. 2007. *Shaping Theology: Engagements in a Religious and Secular World.* Oxford: Blackwell Publishing.

———. 2011. *The Future of Christian Theology.* West Sussex: Wiley-Blackwell.

Harinck, George, and Gerard Dekker. 2007. "The Position of the Church as Institute in Society: A Comparison between Bonhoeffer and Kuyper." *The Princeton Seminary Bulletin* 28, no. 1: 86-98.

Himes, Brant. 2012. "Distinct Discipleship: Abraham Kuyper, Dietrich Bonhoeffer, and Christian Engagement in Public Life." Unpublished paper, Kuyper Center Conference.

Huber, Wolfgang. 1980. "Wahrheit und Existenzform, Anregungen zu einer Theorie der Kirche bei Dietrich Bonhoeffer." In *Konsequenzen: Dietrich Bonhoeffers Kirchenverständnis Heute,* ed. Ernst Feil and Ilse Tödt. München: Kaiser.

Huntemann, Georg. 1989. *Der Andere Bonhoeffer: Die Herausforderung des Modernismus.* Wuppertal: R. Brockhaus.

Luckens, Michael B., Victoria J. Barnett, and Mark S. Brocker. 2012. "Introduction." In *Ecumenical, Academic, and Pastoral Work: 1931-32,* vol. 11 of *Dietrich Bonhoeffer Works,* English Edition, ed. Victoria J. Barnett, Mark S. Brocker, and Michael B. Luckens, trans. Anne Schmidt-Lange et al. Minneapolis: Fortress Press.

Plant, Stephen. 2005. "The Sacrament of Ethical Reality: Dietrich Bonhoeffer on Ethics for Christian Citizens." *Society for Christian Ethics* 18, no. 3: 71-87.

Rasmussen, Larry R. 2009. "Introduction." In *Berlin: 1932-33,* vol. 12 of *Dietrich Bonhoeffer Works,* English Edition, ed. Larry Rasmussen, trans. Isabel Best, David Higgins, and Douglas W. Stott. Minneapolis: Fortress Press.

Strohm, Christoph. 2012. "Afterword." In *Ecumenical, Academic, and Pastoral Work: 1931-32,* vol. 11 of *Dietrich Bonhoeffer Works,* English Edition, ed. Victoria J. Barnett, Mark S. Brocker, and Michael B. Luckens, trans. Anne Schmidt-Lange et al. Minneapolis: Fortress Press.

The Heart of the Academy: Herman Bavinck in Debate with Modernity on the Academy, Theology, and the Church

Marinus de Jong

Science and Religion in the Low Countries between 1903 and 2013

This article deals with a debate between two Dutch theologians on a pair of related issues: the justification of the existence of the Christian academy, and theology's place in the academy. While the debate in question took place more than a hundred years ago, it nonetheless remains highly relevant today.

I will first introduce the matter by means of a contemporary Dutch debate. Following this, the 1903 debate will be dealt with, and concluding remarks offered. These remarks will also focus on the relation of church and academy, the theme of this Kuyper Review. In the debate this relation of church and academy was not the primary issue but, as will be shown, not without relevance to the place of theology in the academy.

In early 2013, Prof. Onno van Schayck, a respected medical scholar in the Netherlands and a Christian, claimed in a personal interview to have witnessed a woman's bone grow after a prayer (Geloof en Wetenschap 2013). He said he had observed this growth of a human bone, which normally could not have happened. Because he could not explain it scientifically, he considered this a miracle. This statement brought about a little riot in the Dutch media.

A provocative reaction on a very impolite but highly popular Dutch news website, geenstijl.nl, reads (Nanninga 2013),

> And what does the University do? Does it gently address Prof. Miracle while accompanying him to a forest environment with kind nurses? . . . No, the University threw on it a really serious little debate on 'Faith and Science'.

> Come on lads. Faith is Faith, otherwise it would have been called 'Certain Knowledge'. Science is saying that someone's stump grew back and then be able to prove it. Such a debate is keeping up the appearance of the legitimacy of completely wacko quackery from the year 1376.

A group of Dutch Christian scholars responded to the various reactions in the media by means of an open letter dated 12 March 2013 in which they asked for freedom of speech for scientists (Bovenberg, Van den Brink, et al. 2013):

> This also leads to the peculiar statement that an academic is not allowed to publicly speculate on possible alternative explanations of otherwise unexplainable observations. Such an approach harms both the academy and the society.

Maarten Keulemans responded in the *Volkskrant,* a Dutch national newspaper, on 13 March 2013, arguing that it has been scientifically proven repeatedly that prayer does not affect illness. His complaint was that people like van Schayck (amongst other Christian scientists) apparently ignore scientific results (Keulemans 2013):

> Science begins with accepting an objective reality outside of us, even if it does not match our experience. Whoever is unable to live up to this principle does not belong to the academy. . . . My plea is for the advancement of good science and simultaneously for the exclusion of faith. If individual academics really need to ignore scientific proof, they are free to go and do something else.

This debate shows how relevant questions around the justification of the existence of Christian scholarship, and the closely related question of theology as part of the academy, are. We now turn to the early twentieth-century debate with these questions in mind.

Herman Bavinck versus Herman Groenewegen

Terminology

Before describing the context of the debate it is important to make some terminological clarifications. The classic problem of how one translates the Dutch term *wetenschap* (and its German cognate, *Wissenschaft*) also occurs in this article. The terms "science" and "scholarship" will be used interchangeably; both refer to the broader sense implied in the word *wetenschap,* i.e., the entire academy, and not only the natural sciences.

In addition to this, Bavinck makes frequent use of the term "positivism." This is to be understood in its broadest sense: knowledge must be founded on experience only and thus implies a rejection of metaphysics. This is the philosophical school associated with Auguste Comte (one of Bavinck's adversaries). The term "modernism" also needs delineation and should be understood according to Abraham Kuyper's use of the term, referring to theological modernism, i.e., liberal Protestantism in the nineteenth century.

The Debate

It is important to understand the debate in its proper context. At the beginning of the twentieth century the so-called *schoolstrijd* was still a major issues in Dutch politics. Initially this "battle" was for the recognition of separate religious primary schools, next to secular state schools, but the discussion also extended to the academy. Therefore a law was designed to enable the recognition of "Extraordinary Universities," universities with a particular worldview or religious foundation. For Kuyper this very concretely meant the recognition of the degrees awarded by the Free University in Amsterdam, founded by Kuyper in 1880. As Prime Minister, Kuyper strove for parliamentary recognition of the degrees awarded by Extraordinary Universities. He finally succeeded in 1905 (Donner 1978: 29-59).

This political debate forms the background to and the occasion for the theological debate between Kuyper's colleague Herman Bavinck (1854-1921) and the Remonstrant modern theologian Herman Groenewegen (1862-1930). Although Bavinck's name and fame have survived into the present, Groenewegen is not particularly well known. This was different during his lifetime. As professor in philosophy of religion at the Remonstrant Seminary in Leiden, he was a widely respected Kant scholar, socially very engaged, and also a popular preacher in the Remonstrant churches (Brugmans et al. 1932: 590). Like Bavinck, he was very active in the church politics of the church to which he belonged (Barnard 2006: 258-66). The large number of newspaper articles prompted by his death are a witness to his stature.[1]

1. Articles relating his death and burial were published in *De Banier* (1930), *Het Nieuwsblad van het Noorden* (1930), and the *Algemeen Handelsblad* (1930).

The subject of the debate was, as can be expected from the political context, the justification of the existence of a distinct Christian academy and thus of theology. At stake, especially for Bavinck, was a public place for theology and Christian scholarship. The debate took place in three publications. First, Bavinck's (1902) inaugural lecture at the Free University, "Godsdienst en Godgeleerdheid" (Religion and Theology), the publication that induced a reaction from Groenewegen; secondly, Groenewegen's (1903) reaction, "Wetenschap of Dogmatisme" (Science or Dogmatism), an article published in the *Theologisch Tijdschrift;* and thirdly, Bavinck's (1904) reply a year later in the booklet *Christelijke Wetenschap* (Christian Science).

The debate is not implicit. They refer to each other explicitly in the footnotes of their publications. As an example of their considerable mutual respect, combined with their maintenance of starkly different positions, we find Groenewegen writing (1903: 396):

> I prefer to refer to the fair and important inaugural lecture held by Dr. Bavinck at the Free University. It is a warm and very serious plea for theological dogmatism. One will find in it many a word sympathetic for its piety and powerful faith, besides the expected disregard for the liberal religion and science. But nowhere is dignity lost from sight, although the appreciation and the understanding of the opponent falls short enormously.

A postcard dated 3 May 1904 in the Bavinck Archives at the Free University proves that Bavinck and Groenewegen did have some correspondence. It reads (Groenewegen 1904):

> I thank you for sending me your book. I am sorry I didn't know of it when I wrote mine, which I also sent you. I would have liked to have answered you in it. Well, the occasion therefore will probably occur. Rest assured I have read yours with interest. Yours Sincerely, your Dr. H. Y. Groenewegen.[2]

On the basis of this historical context, we can now turn to the actual contents of the debate.

2. The handwritten original in Dutch reads: "G.H. Ik dank u voor de toezending van uw boek. Het spijt mij dat ik het niet heb gekend toen ik het mijne schreef, die ik u ook deed toekomen. Ik had er u gaarne in beantwoord. Nu, de gelegenheid zal zich daartoe nog wel voordoen. Wees verzekerd dat ik met belangstelling het uwe heb gelezen. Hoogachtend uw dr. H. Y. Groenewegen."

Epistemology

To understand the arguments in question clearly, various epistemological issues must be taken into consideration. The subsequent discussion of science more generally and finally theology will be based on this.

Bavinck and Groenewegen agree that science obtains knowledge only through empirical observation. However, their approaches diverge soon after. Groenewegen pleads for a strictly objective epistemology: only empirical observation by universal reason is valid scientific observation. The subjective element must be ruled out as much as possible. Failing this, science becomes dogmatism: precisely that from which Immanuel Kant has freed us, argues Groenewegen. He understands that we can never be entirely objective, but nonetheless maintains that the academic should strive for the highest possible levels of objectivity, and that for the sake of the academy and the truth, because only reason is universal. A concept Groenewegen refers to frequently in this context is the *universal life of reason*. This is the Kantian idea that only human reason is trustworthy in acquiring knowledge, owing to its universality. Empirical observation is the foundation, but only with the eye of human reason.

Bavinck does not agree with Groenewegen on this point. Labeling Groenewegen's approach a "positivist epistemology," Bavinck highlights three problems that go some way in summarizing his critique of Groenewegen. First, Bavinck claims, all knowing is subjective. Knowledge is ultimately founded upon the witness of self-consciousness, as he calls it. As a person one has a deep conviction, one's religion, and this ultimately decides everything. It can never be reduced to a private affair *(Privatsache)*. Rather, it is one's foundation *(beginsel)*. There is no such thing as presuppositionless *(voraussetzungslose)* observation, as is claimed by the positivists. We would be wiser to be aware of our presuppositions while practicing science, for they will very likely influence our empirical observations. As such, trying to get rid of our presuppositions in order to be "as objective as possible" is a futile enterprise. According to Bavinck we will never be objective. This should be recognized by those who want to obtain truthful knowledge. It is this objection that is the foundation of Bavinck's conviction that life and science and thus also church and academy should never be separated. We will come back to this below.

Second, he argues, how can you ever be sure there is order in the things you observe? If you want to do academic research, you have to presuppose the existence of order in the things you observe, in addition to presupposing their knowability. Bavinck claims that this presupposition also underlies the positivist epistemology, despite its claims to presuppositionlessness. He identifies this presupposition as the *logos* placed in the creation by God, "that in all the appearances dwells unity, order, thought, *logos,* a *logos* which answers to the *logos* in the human mind" (Bavinck 1904: 37). More fundamentally, he asks, how can we be sure there is a reality outside us at all? This, to Bavinck (1904: 35), is fundamentally a matter of "confidence in God's truthfulness." His assertion, then, is that Groenewegen and the positivist epistemology he represents do not account for such a presupposition and are thus internally inconsistent.

Third, Bavinck argues that positivist epistemology unnecessarily limits reality to the visible realm, without having proper reasons to do so. In fact, it implies the claim that there is a *terra incognita* where knowledge cannot venture. How can they know that? Bavinck asks. And how can they declare something as unknowable if it is unknowable? This is all highly paradoxical and problematic.

So in the end, Bavinck claims, epistemology (and, by import, science) is a deeply subjective matter and rests on many unproven presuppositions. These presuppositions are unavoidable and do not prove problematic as long as one acknowledges their existence and important role. It needs to be accepted that these presuppositions are decided elsewhere, not in science or reason, but in the human heart. And for Bavinck this means that epistemology is primarily a matter of religion. Behind this argument lies the idea that religion is the source and most deciding feature of the human being and of society, an idea comparable with the Dooyeweerdian *grondmotief,* developed in the early twentieth century at the Free University (Dooyeweerd 1959: 8-10).

If religion is the deciding feature, Bavinck continues, and religion is ultimately decided by revelation, the principal epistemological question ultimately becomes: "What do you think of Christ? That was, is and will be the question of the ages" (Bavinck 1904: 88). Which religion you adhere to is decided by which revelation you accept as truthful and authoritative, Bavinck argues (1918: 291-95). Christian revelation culminates in the person of Jesus Christ, and accordingly, one's subjective acceptance or rejection of him will prove fundamental for all of life, notwithstanding the realm of epistemology.

This is a fascinating and typically nineteenth-century neo-Calvinist argument. Most interesting is that Bavinck's critique shows many similarities with classic postmodern critiques of the positivist philosophy of science. This is especially true of Thomas Kuhn's seminal work *The Structure of Scientific Revolutions* (1962), where he asks for a role of history in the philosophy of science. The history of science, he argues, is a history of more or less random paradigm shifts, rather than a history of linear progress, as was (and often is) commonly held. His contemporary Paul Feyerabend (1975) took this further in denying that the entire scientific enterprise is a random historical neutral paradigm shift. Instead, he claims it to be nothing less than a new way of exerting power, and goes as far as labeling it "that most recent, most aggressive and most dogmatic religious institution" (Feyerabend 1975: 15). For Kuhn, and even more so for Feyerabend, there is nothing objective and neutral about science. Although Kuhn is now widely accepted in the philosophy of religion, the public sphere still sees the postivist Groenewegenesque perspective flourishing. In that sphere, science is still deemed objective and is claimed to move in a linear progress. That much seems fairly clear in the aforementioned recent Dutch controversy.[3] As such it indeed behaves as an aggressive dogmatic institution.

The Academy

The way Groenewegen and Bavinck construct their views on the academy flows logically from their prior epistemological commitments. Groenewegen wants science to be free from dogmatism of any kind; it is only empirical observation by universal reason which leads to universal and thus scientific knowledge. Science can never have an epithet; it is either science or nothing at all. "Dogmatism, if you want, is also science, just as a silly verse can be called poetry" (Groenewegen 1903: 387). It is a violation of good science to have dogmatic presuppositions. If we would accept this, everything could be called science, Groenewegen argues. This means that a believer (as Groenewegen considered himself) must be honest and submit his faith to his scientific discoveries, no matter how painful this might be. Ultimately, Groenewegen asserts, he will be richer, because he is closer to the truth, and thus closer to God. Strict empirical observation by universal reason will bring humanity closer to the truth, a path blocked by dogmatism, he argues, as it leads one away from the truth.

This idea receives a similar application to theology, which should never be dogmatic and must thus change into an objective science of religion. It may not restrict its object of study to any specific religion or prior revelation. In practice this "objective" study of all religions led to a view that Christianity is the climax of all religions and modern theology the apex of Christianity. The existence of God was not a matter of debate at all. The science of religion, "which tries to understand the life of religious consciousness, which springs with love and piety from the holy, from God," is considered good by Groe-

3. Cf. also Van den Brink 2004: 174-79.

newegen (1903: 424). This quote betrays a great deal of his presuppositions, to which we will come back below. Groenewegen refutes the accusation that this manner of practicing theology is merely liberal partisanship. He poses the rhetorical question: "Wouldn't neo-Calvinism have earned a public chair long before the foundation of the Free University?" (Groenewegen 1903: 413).

Bavinck would definitely have agreed with him on this point. Early in his career he hoped to take up a position at the Leiden State University as becomes visible when he writes to his friend Snouck-Hurgronje after the Leiden professor of dogmatics, Rauwenhoff, passed away in 1889 (De Bruijn and Harinck 1999: 138):

> I must confess that the chair Rauwenhoff occupied, is appealing to me greatly. I make no illusions concerning the objections, especially the work with my manner of thinking among men who all have another point of view and which many of them also maintain and defend with great scholarly force. Nonetheless such a place does attract me for the great freedom and rich oppurtunity it would offer me to confirm my convictions scientifically and to share them with others.

Bavinck's ideal was a broad University where different schools of thought founded on different *beginsels* could work together and advance science together (Bavinck 1904: 31):

> No modern scholar, who goes with his time and does not lock himself up in his dogmas, will ever devalue studies in philosophy, literature, physics or history by Roman Catholic or Protestant believers. Conversely, Christians have never been so narrow-minded as to reject all scientific research done by unbelievers. . . . For they believe that God, the same God, whom they confess as their Father in Christ, causes his sun to rise on the evil and the good, and sends rain on the righteous and the unrighteous.

Here, the key neo-Calvinist concept of common grace is clearly playing its part, although Bavinck does not name it explicitly. It might have been that Bavinck was not initially keen on the idea of the Free University, and that he in the end chose to leave Kampen for Amsterdam as a lesser of two evils. As a student he had already decided not to study at the small Kampen School of Theology, but at the State University in Leiden. That typifies Bavinck's attitude to the place of theology in the academy.

This attitude, however, was not a surrender to the modern view of science. Bavinck boldly claims a place for a distinctive Christian academy. Different worldviews exist; should they be taken very seriously, good scientific knowledge is likely to develop. Notwithstanding this generous approach, Bavinck is clear on what good science should be: the revelation of God in Christ should be the subjective foundation for epistemology and thus for the academy. From that revelation one can presuppose an orderly *logos* in creation and trust in God that he guides empirical observation to truthful knowledge. In this sense one could say that Bavinck saw all science as Christian, whether its proponents recognize it or not. His argument is that the academy's existence owes a great deal to Christianity, and that it still rests on Christian foundations without which it cannot consistently function. For Bavinck, the entire scientific enterprise of modernists, Catholics and Calvinists alike, is like a living organism that will continue to grow. Here we look a truly turn-of-the-century scholar in the eyes: science is truth-finding and "with the growing of knowledge, adoration will augment likewise. Because all science is the rendering of thoughts that have been put by God in his works" (Bavinck 1904: 58). For Bavinck, science is part of worship; through it we discover more of the beauty of God and his creation. In this view science is not only fundamentally Christian, it is also significant within a theological account of worship.

Theology

For Bavinck, theology is the queen of the academy. On this point, however, Groenewegen and Bavinck disagree strongly. Bavinck argues that theology must be the queen of sciences, or she must disappear from the academy and merge with the faculties of History and Literature. If faith is ruled out beforehand, theology is nothing more than the study of a few specific books and a specific group in history and the present. Here Bavinck sees yet another inconsistency in the modernist approach to the academy. Groenewegen does not want to abandon the separate faculty of theology. Furthermore, he argues that its object should be all religions, and to discover the truth in all of them. This all looks somewhat postmodern, but for Groenewegen it was clear that modern Christianity was the highest form of religion, as has already been shown above. He preached in church regularly and was active within the Remonstrant congregations.

This is precisely what Bavinck (1904: 77) criticizes: "The modern science of religion, which, as a separate faculty, rests on the presupposition of the truth of religion, takes for granted at the same time and in advance the existence, revelation and knowability of God. That is to say, they still stick halfway into metaphysics, and is but partly grown above supernaturalism." Following this, Bavinck alleges that the new science of religion had yet to yield particularly interesting results.

In Bavinck's judgment, the new science of religion engendered a separation between the church and the academy which was harmful for both. In theology this unhealthy rupture is felt most strongly. "Nowhere is this conflict felt with more pain than in the heart of the student who, having grown up in a Christian home, arrives at the gymnasium and the academy and is confronted with modern science" (Bavinck 1902: 13). Bavinck himself had experienced this when he went to study in Leiden. He saw this as applying even more pointedly to ordained ministry within the church, where trained ministers "cannot speak anymore in many cases, because they do not believe. They have nothing left to proclaim, because the power and the glory of the gospel was taken from them by the critique. They can no longer witness, because their childlike trust in the word of the apostles was shocked" (Bavinck 1902: 24). For Bavinck, the academy should not be torn from everyday life, the church should not be distanced from theology, and epistemology should not be removed from the convictions of heart. At this point it becomes clear again that the two issues at stake in this article are indeed interrelated. The justification of Christian scholarship, being the principal issue for Bavinck and Groenewegen, implies, for Bavinck at least, a close connection of church and academy, of academy and life. Life, like God, is one, Bavinck would say, and one thus needs a holistic approach to science that finds its origin in the human heart, in faith. A good theologian is never far from the church; a good scholar takes the whole of life into account.

Concluding Remarks

In exploring the Bavinck-Groenewegen debate, its connections with contemporary issues on theology's place in the academy have been apparent. We will now develop these connections in a more structured way as we come to the conclusion. There are four points where we can connect the debate to today's issues.

Challenge to the Contemporary Conception of Science

First of all, in drawing on their respective contributions in the present day, it must be said that Bavinck makes a strong case against the prevailing philosophy of science, both now and then. In popular culture this has seen little change. Scholars are the pastors of our time; scientists are turned to for the last word. Science means progress and brings us further. It is objectivity and truth, and outside it there is no truth. Such are the creeds of the modern society. In response to this, Bavinck provides clear tools with which to take up a position as Christian scholars in the midst of the academy. His fundamental challenge to the prevailing positivist philosophy of science can still serve present-day Christian academics. It is noteworthy that in more recent currents in the philosophy of science, such as in the works of Thomas Kuhn and Paul Feyerabend, Christian scholars can find allies in challenging the prevailing method. More recently also Jürgen Habermas has emphasized that science can never be free of values (Habermas cited in Van den Brink 2004: 166-67). There are always *Erkentnissinteressen* (knowledge interests) which play their part. Of course, doing science from an explicitly Christian perspective or paradigm is a separate question. Groenewegen also raises a serious question when he says that according to Bavinck's argument, everything could be called science. That having been said, Bavinck raises serious issues for contemporary science: why is metaphysics beyond the reach of the academy? How do we know there is order in reality? How can we be sure of our senses? Perhaps Bavinck is too hasty in asserting that without God these questions cannot be answered. His questions, however, are nonetheless useful in tempering the condescension often found in contemporary science.

Engagement with Science

A second, related notion is that Bavinck shows the importance of science and the place of Christians and theologians within it. The practice of science is of utmost importance. For Bavinck, as has been said, science is a form of worship in its discovery of more about God through his creation. Bavinck is perhaps overly optimistic on this point. Indeed, his position almost looks like natural theology where the disastrous effects of the fall seem not always to be accounted for. The underlying concept of common grace is very important in Bavinck's positive attitude towards science in general. Karl Barth's radical critique of nineteenth-century theology, especially when God is too easily connected with this world, also applies to Bavinck's optimistic view of the academy. The concept of scientific progress, clearly present in Bavinck's account, has also been profoundly challenged from another side by, for example, Thomas Kuhn. Nonetheless, I believe academic work can be a form of worship and as such, it is important that Christians participate in it to discover more of the riches of God's creation and to account for this accordingly.

Theology in the Public Sphere

Third, closely related to the previous point is Bavinck's challenge to be present as Christians in the academy. Bavinck does not want to abandon science to the positivists. Indeed, Bavinck wants to be present in the secular academy and does not want to be excluded to the ghetto of the private sphere. As was mentioned previously, his life — particularly the contexts in which he studied and worked — bears witness to this attitude. Once he got a position at the Free University, he kept engaging in debate with the modern theologians, of which the debate with Groenewegen is a clear example. He earned the respect of the "secular" scholars by his sound scholarship and honest attitude. And as such he overtly claimed a place for theology in the academy and argued for a distinctively Christian perspective in the midst of dominant modernist and secular perspectives. This was grounded in the idea that a Christian *beginsel* will give other insights, foremost in theology, but also in other disciplines.

Church and Academy

In conclusion, Bavinck suggests that life and academy need to be connected. (This principle finds a ready application in the relationship of theology and the church.) To draw on a Dutch expression, the scholar remains a human being and he needs to have his feet firmly in the clay (Bavinck 1918: 662). I think Groenewegen was also convinced by this same fact. He was a man of the church. At his funeral a colleague remarked of him: "He was a great preacher and he knew how to popularize science" (Algemeen Handelsblad 1930). And another colleague, Prof. Heering, said: "A man, touched by God and therefore bound to testify of Him, has left us" (Algemeen Handelsblad 1930). Despite his commitment to doing this, he did not want to take the consequences for his epistemology and for his concept of theology, for the sake of the universality of reason. It is interesting that, once again, the philosopher Feyerabend (1975: 11) makes a similar point to Bavinck:

> Scientific education . . . simplifies science by simplifying its participants: first a domain of research is defined, the domain is separated from the rest

> of history and given a logic of its own. Thorough training in such a logic then conditions those working in the domain; it makes their actions more uniform and it freezes large parts of the historical process as well. Stable "facts" arise and persevere despite the vicissitudes of history. . . . A person's religion for example or his metaphysics, or his sense of humour (his natural sense of humour and not the inbred and always rather nasty kind of jocularity one finds in specialized professions) must not have the slightest connections with his scientific activity.

Academy and life, theology and the church, need each other. This connection is the logical consequence of Bavinck's subjective epistemology. This is how the main topic of the justification of Christian scholarship asks for a holistic integration of church and academy, life and science. Science should not and cannot become an entity separated from daily life or it risks losing relevance altogether. Theology should serve the church or it risks losing its right to exist. Without that, theology is bound to dissolve into history and sociology. The distinct voice of theology can only be heard from faith in Christ and in the church (cf. Barth 1963: 167 and Bavinck 1918: 22-26). This, and I quote Bavinck (1904: 59), is "because our spirit, because the world, because God is one."

BIBLIOGRAPHY

Algemeen Handelsblad. 1930. "Begrafenis — prof. Groenewegen." *Algemeen Handelsblad,* 13 April, p. 10.

Barnard, Tjaard. 2006. *Van "verstoten kind" tot belijdende kerk: De Remonstrantse Broederschap tussen 1850 en 1940.* Amsterdam: De Bataafse Leeuw.

Barth, Karl. 1963. *Church Dogmatics* I/2. Edinburgh: T&T Clark.

Bavinck, H. 1902. *Godsdienst en godgeleerdheid.* Wageningen: N. V. Drukkerij "Vada."

———. 1904. *Christelijke Wetenschap.* Kampen: J. H. Kok.

———. 1918. *Gereformeerde Dogmatiek.* Part 1. Kampen: J. H. Kok.

Bovenberg, Lans, Gijsbert Van den Brink, et al. 2013. *Open Brief: Bevorder goede wetenschap en gun wetenschappers hun persoonlijke vrijheid.* Available online at http://www.geloofenwetenschap.nl/index.php/nieuws/item/download/56.html [Accessed 29 August 2013].

Brugmans, H., J. H. Scholten, and P. Kleintjes, eds. 1932. *Gedenkboek van het Athenaeum en de Universiteit van Amsterdam, 1632-1932.* Amsterdam: Stadsdrukkerij.

De Banier. 1930. "Prof. Dr. H. IJ. Groenewegen." *De Banier: Staatkundig gereformeerd dagblad,* 11 April.

De Bruijn, J., and G. Harinck, eds. 1999. *Een Leidsche vriendschap: De briefwisseling tussen Herman Bavinck en Christiaan Snouck Hurgronje, 1875-1921*. Baarn: Ten Have.

Donner, J. 1978. *De Vrijheid van het bijzonder wetenschappelijk onderwijs*. Zwolle: W. E. J. Tjeenk Willink.

Dooyeweerd, H. 1959. *Vernieuwing en bezinning: Om het reformatorisch grondmotief.* Zutphen: Van den Brink & Co.

Feyerabend, Paul. 1975. *Against Method*. London: Verso.

Geloof en Wetenschap. 2013. *Waarom is er ziekte als God er is?* Available online at http://www.geloofenwetenschap.nl/index.php/videoaudio/item/320-waarom-is-er-ziekte-als-god-er-is?.html [Accessed 29 August 2013].

Groenewegen, H. IJ. 1903. "Wetenschap of dogmatisme." *Theologisch Tijdschrift* 37: 385-424.

———. 1904. "H. IJ. Groenewegen to H. Bavinck" (letter). *Archief Bavinck*. 7. Amsterdam: Historisch Documentatie Centrum.

Keulemans, Maarten. 2013. "Christenwetenschappers, ik gun jullie de vrijheid iets anders te gaan doen." *De Volkskrant*, 13 March.

Kuhn, Thomas. 1962. *The Structure of Scientific Revolutions*. Chicago: University of Chicago Press.

Nanninga, A. 2013. *Uni Maastricht met één been in gekkenhuis*. Available online at http://www.geenstijl.nl/mt/archieven/2013/02/weg_met_uni_maastricht_het_is.html [Accessed 29 August 2013].

Nieuwsblad. 1930. "Prof. Dr. H. IJ. Groenewegen†." *Nieuwsblad van het Noorden*, 11 April, p. 21.

Van den Brink, Gijsbert. 2004. *Een publieke zaak: Theologie tussen geloof en wetenschap*. Zoetermeer: Boekencentrum.

Not without the Church as Institute: The Relevance of Abraham Kuyper's Ecclesiology for Christian Public and Theological Responsibilities in the Twenty-first Century

Ad de Bruijne

Introduction

In many countries attention to the public responsibility of churches and Christians appears to be on the rise (Jenkins 2002; Katongole 2005; Bretherton 2010; Kennedy 2010; Helms 2012; Sider 2012). In Western societies, this attention is caused by ongoing secularization. Here the key question is how Christians should respond to a situation in which the Christian tradition is no longer dominant. In some non-Western countries it is the increase in the number of Christians that nurtures similar reflection. There the key question is whether and how Christians should make use of the growing opportunities for public influence. This paper investigates how the ecclesiology of Abraham Kuyper could contribute to this contemporary reflection on the public responsibility of the church in various contexts.[1] First an outline will be offered of a current Western debate. Second, the contextual nature of Kuyper's ecclesiology will be uncovered. Third, his distinction between the church as an organism and the church as an institution will be reinterpreted. Finally, Kuyper's vision will be applied to present-day contexts. It will be contended that the church in its institutional dimension is indispensable to Christian public action, and that this institutionality is liturgically determined.

1. For a thorough treatment of Kuyper's ecclesiology that acknowledges its importance for his public philosophy, see Wood 2013.

Two Christian Positions

Among Western Christians two opposing positions on the relationship between church and state can be distinguished (De Bruijne 2006; 2012). Both reject the dominant liberal paradigm which confines religion to the private sphere. They differ, however, about the extent to which church and Christians may adapt themselves to modern liberal society. The first position presents the Christian faith as useful and relevant in the public domain and aspires to influence society. Christian convictions are translated into generally accepted notions while the church itself is restricted to the private sphere. Christianity more or less functions as "civil religion" (Shanks 1995). The second view presents the church as a contrast society, which should be publicly different. The church does not strive for power or influence, but exists as an exemplary community that bears witness and experiences suffering (Hauerwas and Willimon 1989).[2] These different positions are relevant not only to the political sphere but also to other areas of public life. They define, for example, the debate on the public status of theology. The first approach prefers a general scientific context for theology, while the second locates theology primarily in the context of the church as an alternative public community (Murphy 1996; De Bruijne 2004; Van den Brink 2004; D'Costa 2005).

The difference between these two positions is largely rooted in ecclesiology. Different views on the church lead to divergent visions on the public calling of Christians (Wood 2013: 174). These not only concern the question of the importance of the church, but also touch upon its institutional structures. If the church is conceived as a worldwide empire, as has been done for Roman Catholicism, its public theology will develop differently than if it is seen as a national entity or as a denominational group of local communities. In the same way contemporary tendencies toward de-institutionalization, as can be noticed in "emerging" churches, have corresponding consequences for their public stance (Murray 2004: 252-85; Mannion 2007).

Kuyper on the "Colony of Heaven"

The contemporary debate could profit from the ecclesiology of Abraham Kuyper. At first glance, Kuyper's view resembles that of scholars who demonstrate the societal relevance of Christianity. He distinguishes between the

2. For a comparison between Kuyper and Hauerwas, see Chung 1999.

church as institution and the church as organism. Apparently, the institute should keep its distance from the public domain. The organism, on the other hand, has to fulfill responsibilities in all spheres of life. In these it constitutes communal Christian life by establishing Christian organizations to influence the public domain. Upon closer inspection, however, Kuyper's vision approaches near the second contemporary position. It is remarkable how often Kuyper criticizes the synthesis between church and politics that had developed since Constantine the Great (1872: 12; 1873a: 20; 1898: 87f.; 1905: 125; 1911-1912: I.262, 266; 1916: 475; 1931-1932: II.261, III.207ff.). Sometimes, reading Kuyper is like hearing the kind of grumbling on "Constantinianism" that characterizes the writings of Yoder or Hauerwas (Wright 2000; Hauerwas and Willimon 1996: 25). Also striking is a characterization of the church in a lecture that Kuyper presented on the occasion of the seventh annual meeting of his Amsterdam Free University. In it Kuyper calls the church a "colony of heaven" (1887: 32). Exactly the same expression is found in the works of Hauerwas (Hauerwas and Willimon 1989). So, with whom would Kuyper side today?

Kuyper's speech from which the expression "colony of heaven" is taken bears the title "Twofold Homeland." According to Kuyper, Christians are citizens of two homelands simultaneously: the heavenly and the earthly. They belong to the earthly homeland through their birth from earthly parents, while their place in the heavenly homeland is the consequence of their rebirth from the heavenly Father. This earthly homeland Kuyper considers as not natural. In creation God mirrored his divine "life" in humanity (1911: I.337; 1931-1932: I.412, II.363, 645, 650, 653). That life was both one and infinitely varied. God's original plan was to let the human reflection of his life develop from the basic creational order of the family into a multitude of spheres on a global scale, which would still remain perfectly united. During this process, creation would be fully developed. God intended a pluriform global society of which he himself would be king. Separate nations and states with their own governments did not fit into that picture and became necessary only because of the Fall. Under the conditions of sin, this expanding global society would cause a concentration of evil and anti-divine power. This posed a threat to the intended diversity of life and the unfolding of creation, because it implied an unnatural uniformity. As an answer to that and only for the duration of history, God divided the world into a multitude of nations and separate political entities. He created an artificial multiplicity to avoid this harmful uniformity. This artificial multiplicity ensured the development of the originally intended multiplicity under the conditions of sin.[3] So, according to Kuyper, the existence of earthly homelands and the fact that every human being is a citizen of one of these constitute a temporary divine measure of common grace and not a natural anthropological reality.

Moreover, God made a new beginning based upon his gift of particular grace. In Christ he communicates new life for the new humanity that will inhabit his future world. In this new creation the fruits of common grace will be incorporated. The artificial division of humankind will no longer be necessary. Separate nations and governments will have had their day. God's worldwide kingdom will take their place, hosting a perfect creational diversity. The heavenly homeland forms the start of that coming kingdom. The church in turn consists of the community of citizens of this heavenly homeland. They share in Christ's new life and are called by God to advance this life on earth. Kuyper even characterizes regeneration as "the invisible commencement of a heavenly country." Fallen creation has to be recaptured. So, citizens of the heavenly homeland should acknowledge an earthly vocation. The new life will "wrestle itself through the seams of fallen creation." Christians not only have to reckon with God's particular grace but also with God's common grace. They must acknowledge their citizenship in an earthly homeland. So the church forms a "colony of heaven," with a vocation in, as Kuyper says, a foreign earthly country (1870a: 19; 1870b: 12, 18f.; 1873a: 8; 1884: 13, 57; 1887: 14f.; 1905: 111-16; 1911-1912: III.259ff.; 1916: 418f.).

Truth in "Moderates" and "Anabaptists"

Now it should not be forgotten that Kuyper developed this position as an alternative to two already existing approaches in his nineteenth-century Dutch context: the "moderate" and the "Anabaptist" options. Remarkably, these two nineteenth-century positions resemble the two contemporary strands of thought about the church's public calling that were mentioned earlier. "Moderates" as well as "Anabaptists" in fact threatened Kuyper's public efforts, including his ambitions with the Free University, which this lecture was to endorse. "Moderates" rejected separate Christian community formation in the various spheres of life. According to them, the existing national structures

3. This contention rests on an interpretation of a seemingly contradictory treatment of plurality in Kuyper, which at one point seems to refer to creational variation and at another to the measures God took upon the fall into sin. See Ad de Bruijne, "'Colony of Heaven': Kuyper's Ecclesiology in the Twenty-first Century" (forthcoming).

of the Netherlands sufficed. This also counted for science and theology, for which state universities offered enough possibilities. Kuyper judged that Moderates forgot the difference between the earthly and the heavenly homeland (1887: 29). Anabaptists, on the other hand, failed to do justice to the fact that the earthly homeland, too, is willed by God. With contemporary debates in mind, it strikes today's reader that Kuyper clearly shows more sympathy for the Anabaptists than for the Moderates. With the Anabaptists he shares the conviction that the citizenship of the heavenly fatherland is decisive. He even exclaims that "so very much in their position is attractive!" With romantic pathos he depicts Christians as pilgrims with a poignant homesickness, singing the chorus "come Lord, come quickly" (1887: 27ff.; 1931-1932: III.17). Also his characterization of the church as a "colony of heaven" fits this inclination. At the same time, however, Kuyper corrects the "Anabaptist" paradigm by stating that the heavenly colony still has to perform a "formidable task" on earth. He refers to Christian efforts in all areas of life and to the organizations that serve these (1887: 38ff.; 1899: 116; 1905: 124; 1911-1912: 105). Between the lines, of course, one hears a passionate plea to support his Free University. So in the end Kuyper develops a third way between the existing alternatives of his day.

Nevertheless, Kuyper's model should not be interpreted as timeless and suitable to all situations. Kuyper deliberately developed it for the Dutch context of his day. He even hints at the fact that in other times his model would turn out differently. Social historians have shown how contextual and strategic Kuyper's choices were (Augustijn and Vree 1998). Unfortunately, they sometimes tend to stress this insight by simultaneously downplaying the role of Kuyper's theological convictions and even criticizing their consistency. A better way would be to recognize that Kuyper's theological basics themselves deliberately let room for diverse applications in various contexts. About Moderates as well as Anabaptists he explicitly states that in other circumstances their choices might be appropriate (1887: 20-26, 31-35, 37; 1907: 52-56; 1931-1932: III.211-17). What Moderates advocate could be possible if a nation's population would consist largely of Christians. Then the church would coincide with the people and the institutions of the earthly homeland would be sufficient for its vocation. In fact, this would come down to a theocratic model in which the earthly homeland and its government cooperates with the church, and contrary to some quick judgments about Kuyper, he certainly is not only critical about that. He even praises theocracy as "this only true idea" (1887: 31). Such an ideal constellation, he claims, once existed in seventeenth-century Holland and again developed in several states in the United States of his day (1873b: 8f.; 1887: 33; 1907: 81; 1916: vii-xii).

On the other hand, according to Kuyper, in the future the Anabaptist public strategy will become inevitable. From the Bible he concludes that the Western world is heading for "frightening days." In their earthly fatherlands, Christians will be refused public space. Christian community formation in the various areas of life will become difficult or even impossible. That leaves the colony of heaven in the earthly homeland in the position of a witnessing and suffering "contrast-community." God will even have to take her up into heaven temporarily (1911-1912: III.76, 225f., 272, 310-13, 350-53; 1931-1932: I.254, 503ff., II.183f., 604-14, 619-23, 634, 668-71). Kuyper seriously considers whether modern secularization might already indicate the commencement of that future. He states that his own days experience the "release of the demons" and therefore are a "hard time." In that case, already in his own days, he would have adopted a more Anabaptist strategy. Nevertheless, his conclusion is that this future is "not yet" imminent, and there are "still" possibilities left. Only because of very specific speculation about the historical vocation of Calvinism under God's providence does he dare to expect delay and even some reversal in the process of de-Christianization. Calvinism, in his view, will reach its climax in twentieth-century America. Only after that will the eschatological battle and God's final judgment follow. It is in the wake of this upcoming American era that he dares to express hope for prolonged blessings to the Netherlands. He even states that such courage would be unjustified for other countries, like Spain or Belgium (1887: 37f.). This proves that he himself did not intend his model to be universal and timeless. His public theology consciously aimed at the unique context of incipient Dutch secularization. Therefore, Kuyper's model is not to be simply transferred to other contexts. Before one implements his theological basics one must analyze other contexts. Only then would the appropriate public theology follow from Kuyper's ecclesiology.

Organism and Institute

But before we do so, we should investigate how this contextuality affects the interpretation of Kuyper's well-known distinction between the church as organism and as institution. Kuyper's preference appears to be for the church as organism, as most interpreters notice. With strategic genius he is seen to adjust the institute to modern society by placing it more or less in the private sphere, but then to recover the public impact of the church in the form of the organism. This organism is the new humanity which conquers all areas of created life for the kingdom of Christ, while the institute is only a temporary, unnatural aid because of sin. Some even argue that Kuyper's commitment to the church as institution was actually driven by his public ambitions for the church as organism (Mouw 2011: 55).

However, Kuyper's theological biography points into another direction. Already in the *Commentatio,* written in his student days, he embraced Schleiermacher's concept of the "organic." Kuyper joined nineteenth-century idealism in the conviction that the institutional church will find its destiny in the modern state and so become superfluous (Vree and Zwaan 2005b: 293 [par. 167],[4] 334-341 [par. 188-91], 352f. [par. 200], 362 [par. 205]; Kuyper 1873a: 6; 1870b: 7; Faber 2010: 183). The young Kuyper clearly considered the institutional church to be relative. But after his conversion to Calvinism, this changed. Then he praises Calvin as the founder of a church, and he develops an authentic passion for the reformation of the institute (1870a: 5, 24; 1870b: 5-7, 18f., 21, 28ff., 32; 1873a: 31, 35; 1884: 14, 16, 135, 178, 195f.; 1905: 109f., 136; Augustijn and Vree 1998: 14). He no longer believes that the institute could already disappear during history. Until the *eschaton* (the last day) the church as organism cannot exist without the institute. This change is reflected in his characterization of the church as "colony of heaven." Supposing that in the preceding sections the conclusion that this expression lies near to Kuyper's heart was correct, then the church as institute must be of great importance to him. Without it the "colony" would dissolve in earthly life and cease to be a colony. It is the twentieth-century perspective that causes modern interpreters to find Kuyper's focus in the organism. Since the nineteenth century, moderns were used to conceive of the church as an institution and they therefore experienced this organic aspect as an innovation. But Kuyper's own development had taken the opposite course. To him the organic character of the church had always been obvious, and he merely rediscovered the importance of the institutional dimension.

It should be remembered that not only "organism" but also "institution" is a typically nineteenth-century concept. With many of his contemporaries, Kuyper believed that as soon as humans consciously interfere with it, organic life will always take on institutional character (Kuyper 1870b: 12, 16f.; 1931-1932: 102f.). But in his first period he judged the institutions of modern civil society to be sufficient for the organic church, while after his conversion he learned to acknowledge the enduring necessity of a distinctive institutionality. The church does not coincide with the institutions of the nation, as former theocrats or

4. ". . . in christianorum mutua in Christo consociatione et conglutinatione arctissima vim insitam ecclesiae retexit."

contemporary moderates claimed, nor should it be kept away from modern society, as the Anabaptist model required. Instead, Kuyper now conceived of the church as a separate institution on the level of civil society. Already this change, and not just his concept of organism, created a new public place for the church in the modern context. From now on, the church belongs to the institutions of modernity. This helps to preserve its identity as colony of heaven and at the same time to take up the above-mentioned "formidable task" in the earthly homeland.

This conclusion implies that one should keep organism and institute together when interpreting Kuyper's ecclesiology. Superficial impressions of Kuyper suggest that the organism would be outside the institute, and that the institute is not organic. But the first and decisive context in which the new organic life exists is the institute. Only after that does this possibly spread to other societal institutions. As already argued, this expansion, according to Kuyper, will not occur in every context, and ultimately only the institute will remain as shelter for the church's organic life (1870b: 15, 30; 1884: 16, 21; 1911-1912: I.44, 70, 82ff., II.122; 1931-1932: II.673, 689). The interpretation of Kuyper's ecclesiology should not depend on its contingent nineteenth-century applications. In the Dutch context of an only incipient secularization and with the promise of a once more flourishing Calvinism, the church as organism could disperse far beyond the institute. But this contingent blessing should not cloud the acknowledgment of the central importance of this institute in Kuyper's ecclesiology. Once secularization continues, his church doctrine would require a concentration of Christian community life around the institute. In the light of proposals by contemporary neo-Calvinists to improve on Kuyper's model, this conclusion proves intriguing. They advocate a closer relationship between Christian public action and the church as institution (Mouw 2011: 99-104). Their plea can be shared, but at the same time it can be contended that this is not an improvement on Kuyper, but concurs with his own ecclesiological intentions.

The Public Character of Theology

Kuyper's ecclesiology contains, for example, implications for the — nowadays much discussed — public character of theology. Kuyper distinguished two possible contexts for doing theology. First, theology can be at home in a seminary supervised by the church and meant to educate new pastors, in line with the biblical principle that it is the task of already-serving pastors to train a new generation of pastors. In this context he locates the classic fourth office in the Reformed church, namely the "doctors" (elders and deacons in addition to ministers). He clearly distinguishes these "doctors" from those who bear the comparable title in the context of a university. Theology, in this church-based, seminary context, should not be treated as a scientific activity in its own right but as an aid for an adequate training of pastors. It is not the task of the institutional church to undertake scientific activities.

The second context in which theology finds its place is the university. As far as theology belongs to the sphere of science, its home lies there. This sphere of science forms a creational terrain that is independent from the institutional church. However, Kuyper proposes a constellation in which professors of theology at a university additionally also receive a church-based appointment as "doctor" in the context of the institutional church, so that new ministers could be educated at the university as well. Faculties of theology would be wise to cooperate with the church when looking for new professors (1884: 64; 1899: 114f.; 1908-1909: II.542-44).

Transposed to contemporary discussions about the public character of theology and its relations to both church and the scientific community, Kuyper's position at first sight supports a clearly public theology, which finds its natural home in the university and not in the church. However, it should not be forgotten that Kuyper does not refer to a general university context but to his Christian Free University, which displays Christian community formation in the field of science. In line with the interpretation of his ecclesiology as developed above, such a Christian university is to be interpreted as an extension of the organic church outside the institute. It penetrates the creational sphere of science. According to Kuyper, the church as institute from the root of its own new life calls forth a new Christian sphere of science (1870b: 17). Seen in this light, it can equally well be contended that Kuyper related theology as public phenomenon to the institutional church, although in a more indirect way.

According to the interpretation in the preceding paragraphs, in other contexts Kuyper's basic notions would require other practical applications and constellations. For example, in a fully Christian society Christian science and theology would possibly be at home in a general university, while on the other hand, in a completely un-Christian society, even a Christian university would be impossible. To remain true to its public character, theology would then have to find a place under the wings of the — in its core — public institution of the church itself. This would not be the optimum, according to Kuyper, but in the given circumstances it would be better than a version of theology that remains public within the context of a university but at the cost of becoming secularized or syncretistic. In many contemporary Western countries a dilemma like this is not just a theoretical one. Kuyper's ecclesiology, at least, provides stimulating lines of thought for a contextually conscious consideration of these questions.

Three Different Contemporary Contexts

With these remarks about theology as public phenomenon we have made a start in applying Kuyper's ecclesiology to contemporary contexts. In so doing, we should make a distinction between the contexts of the Netherlands, the United States, and non-Western emerging Christian nations.

In the Netherlands, after almost a century of renewed Christian public influence, secularization has advanced progressively. The Christian character of many of Kuyper's societal organizations were diluted, and even the institutional churches themselves were affected by this development. Moreover, today no longer a principled but an individualized consumerist version of pluralism has developed, in which the Kuyperian model does not fit easily. Besides, the secular majority appears to have experienced Kuyperianism as a Christian exercise of power, and, resenting this, it viciously attacks the Kuyperian Christian Netherlands. This has become clear especially in many works of literary and musical art (Cliteur 1996; Sengers 2005). Today, Kuyper himself would no longer expect a period of Christian flourishing for the Netherlands, so that the predicted time of an inevitably closer connection between Christian public action and the church as institution seems to be imminent.

The United States today probably finds itself in a situation of incipient secularization comparable to that of the Netherlands in Kuyper's time (Monsma and Soper 2008). Having less of a tradition of Christian public organizations, the United States could still profit from Kuyper's third way between Moderates and Anabaptists. However, Kuyper does not allow for a new bearer of Christian culture following the American era. So from his perspective there seems less reason to expect that America's de-Christianization process could also be reversed or slowed down. Almost certainly Kuyper would interpret the rise of China as a sign of the upcoming final battle (Jacques 2012). Lacking Kuyper's speculative certainties, American Christians at least would be wise to connect ambitions for the building of a Christian public community to the institutional church. Moreover, the Dutch experience presents an unmistakable warning about the risk that well-meant Christian public action still would be perceived as exercise of power.

The same warning counts for non-Western, potentially Christian countries, although Kuyper's philosophy of history, as was shown above, leaves no room for future Christian concentrations of power in non-Western contexts. Here too, reasons exist for proposing a close connection between Christian public activity and the institutional church. Often, Western-like wariness about possible intermingling of religion and public life is absent, while at the same time other religions do not hesitate to be present in public life (Ellis and Ter Haar 1998; Sanneh and Carpenter 2005). Why then should the church hide behind derived forms of Christian communal action? On the other hand, in non-democratic nations Kuyper's vision could possess extra potential, because even then Christian community-building on the level of civil society would offer a way to be publicly significant. However, also civil society is a Western concept. Before implementing Kuyperianism in any society the latter should be acknowledged in its own character.

Institutionality in an Age of Deinstitutionalization

The accent on the church as institute seems to contradict the present postmodern trend towards deinstitutionalization, with its accompanying celebration of authenticity and organic spontaneity. Upon closer inspection, however, this trend should be interpreted primarily as resistance to the static, bourgeois, and bureaucratic kind of institutions of modernity (Haferkamp and Smelser 1992; Zijderveld 2000: 13-15). Kuyper even stimulates an appreciation of this trend, as also for him the new communal life in Christ is foremost an organic reality. At the same time, however, Kuyper could rescue contemporary Christians from the romantic illusion that organic church life could exist without institutionality. And yet, there is no reason to restrict this institutionality to its usual but contingent nineteenth-century forms. The successive institutional church forms have always reflected the varying positions of the church in changing societal contexts (Koffeman and Witte 2001; Dulles 2002; Van den Brink and Van der Kooi 2012: 525ff.). The dominant medieval world church took up the features of an empire. The subsequent theocratic Protestant churches organized themselves nationally. The churches from the incipient era of secularization, individualization, and pluralization became denominations with the institutional features of modern civil society. Again, the present globalized and ever-changing network society, with minority churches that endeavor to influence without exercising power, asks for adequate new institutional forms. Combined with Kuyper's vision on the pluriformity of the institutional church, these insights could lead to an appreciation of some of the emerging new church forms of today.

Liturgy as Ecclesiological Secret

In the preceding sections we found that Kuyper characterized the church as a "colony of heaven" living in a foreign earthly country, which yet has to bear public responsibilities there. With this characterization Kuyper created a third way between the existing alternatives in his nineteenth-century context, namely Moderates and Anabaptists, while at the same time incorporating truth elements of both. It was also shown that already to Kuyper himself, despite his contextually colored use of the possibilities of the church as organism, the church as institute was more decisive than is often recognized. Besides, we contended that Kuyper's model deliberately aimed at a situation of the incipient Dutch secularization, in which he still saw promising perspectives for Calvinism and much Christian potential on the level of society. Today his concepts would have to result in practical models for the public calling of the church, which differ from his organic nineteenth-century forms, especially because of a necessarily more central position for the institutional church. Yet, we allowed for the insight that today institutionality itself too, while being indispensable, could take on new and perhaps more flexible forms.

This, finally, raises the question: On what conditions is it justified to define as church any of those organic, flexible Christian communities that emerge in the public domain today? Kuyper would consider the presence of the ministry of the word as decisive, as it produces regeneration and nurtures the born-again life (1870b: 15; 1887: 16; 1931-1932: III.128). Related to this he confined the special institutionality of the church to history, for in the eschatological future regeneration is no longer needed. Building on many others, the proposal of the present article would be to consider the liturgical reality of "calling upon the name of the Lord" as decisive (Trimp 1983; Landman 1995; Volf 1998; Cavanaugh 2002; Wannenwetsch 2004; Smith 2009; Van den Brink and Van der Kooi 2012: 518f., 537). In so doing, a community takes part in the heavenly liturgy of the ecumenical church of all ages that has approached God's heavenly throne.[5] However variable and flexible organic Christian community formation may be, this liturgical core is indispensable. Thus the church as institution becomes even more important than it was to Kuyper. For even in the eschato-

5. Hebrews 12:22-24; Revelation 14:1-3.

logical future the new humanity will not do without this worship.[6] It remains the heart of all creational Christian communal life. So, against Kuyper but in keeping with Augustine, it can be contended that even in the *eschaton* the specific institutionality of the church will not be fulfilled in other structures of organic life (Augustine 1998: introduction, XI.1, XIV.28, XIX.11, 17, 26). To the contrary, organic Christian life, then spread over all created realms, will appear to be possible only because of this liturgical and therefore institutional center.

REFERENCES

Augustijn, C., and J. Vree. 1998. *Abraham Kuyper: Vast en veranderlijk; De ontwikkeling van zijn denken.* Zoetermeer: Boekencentrum.

Augustine. 1998. *The City of God against the Pagans,* ed. and trans. R. W. Dyson. Cambridge: Cambridge University Press.

Bretherton, Luke. 2010. *Christianity and Contemporary Politics: The Conditions and Possibilities of Faithful Witness.* Chichester: Wiley-Blackwell.

Cavanaugh, William T. 2002. *Theopolitical Imagination.* London: T&T Clark.

D'Costa, Gavin. 2005. *Theology in the Public Square: Church, Academy and Nation.* Malden, MA: Blackwell Publishing.

Chung, Kwang-Duck. 1999. *Ecclesiology and Social Ethics: A Comparative Study of the Social and Ethical Life of the Church in the Views of Abraham Kuyper and Stanley Hauerwas.* Kampen: Van den Berg.

Cliteur, P. B., et al. 1996. *Cultuur, politiek en christelijke traditie: Welke plaats is er voor het christelijke verhaal in onze samenleving?* Baarn: Callenbach.

De Bruijne, A. L. Th., ed. 2004. *Gereformeerde theologie vandaag.* Barneveld: De Vuurbaak.

———. 2006. *Levend in Leviatan: Een onderzoek naar de theorie over "christendom" in de politieke theologie van Oliver O'Donovan.* Kampen: Kok.

———. 2012. "A Banner That Flies Across This Land . . . An Interpretation and Evaluation of Dutch Evangelical Political Awareness since the End of the 20th Century." In *Evangelical Theology in Transition,* ed. C. van der Kooi, E. van Staalduine-Sulman, and A. W. Zwiep, pp. 86-130. Amsterdam: VU University Press.

Dronkers, Pieter. 2012. *Faithful Citizens: Civic Allegiance and Religious Loyalty in a Globalized Society: A Dutch Case Study.* Groningen: Protestantse Theologische Universiteit.

Dulles, Robert Avery. 2002. *Models of the Church.* Expanded edition. [Kindle edition.] Available at: http://www.amazon.com [Accessed 12 February 2014].

6. Revelation 5:13.

Ellis, Stephen, and Gerrie Ter Haar. 1998. "Religion and Politics in Sub-Saharan Africa." *The Journal of Modern African Studies* 36, no. 2: 175-201.

Faber, Riemer. 2010. Review of *Abraham Kuyper's* Commentatio *(1860): The Young Kuyper about Calvin, à Lasco, and the Church.* Vol. 1, *Introduction, Annotations, Bibliography, and Indices;* Vol. 2, *Commentatio.* Ed. Jasper Vree and Johan Zwaan. Brill's Series in Church History. Leiden: Brill.

Haferkamp, Hans, and Neil J. Smelser, eds. 1992. *Social Change and Modernity.* Berkeley: University of California Press.

Hauerwas, Stanley, and William H. Willimon. 1989. *Resident Aliens: Life in the Christian Colony.* Nashville: Abingdon Press.

Hauerwas, Stanley, and William H. Willimon. 1996. *Where Resident Aliens Live: Exercises for Christian Practice.* Nashville: Abingdon Press.

Helms, Eilert. 2011. *Kirche in der Gesellschaft.* Tübingen: Mohr-Siebeck.

Jacques, Martin. 2012. *When China Rules the World: The End of the Western World and the Birth of a New Global Order.* 2nd ed. New York: Penguin Books.

Jenkins, Philip. 2002. *The Next Christendom: The Coming of Global Christianity.* Oxford: Oxford University Press.

Katongole, Emmanuel M. 2005. *A Future for Africa: Critical Essays in Christian Social Imagination.* Scranton: University of Scranton Press.

Kennedy, James C. 2010. *Stad op een berg: De publieke rol van protestantse kerken.* Zoetermeer: Boekencentrum.

Koffeman, Leo J., and Henk Witte, eds. 2011. *Of All Times and of All Places: Protestants and Catholics on the Church Local and Universal.* Zoetermeer: Boekencentrum.

Kuyper, Abraham. 1870a. *Conservatisme en Orthodoxie: Afscheidsrede Utrecht.* Amsterdam: De Hoogh.

———. 1870b. *Geworteld en Gegrond: De kerk als organisme en instituut.* Amsterdam: De Hoogh.

———. 1872. *"Bekeert U, want het Koninkrijk Gods is nabij!"* Amsterdam: De Hoogh.

———. 1873a. *Eenheid.* Amsterdam: De Hoogh.

———. 1873b. *Vrijheid.* Amsterdam: De Hoogh.

———. 1884. *Tractaat van de reformatie der kerken, aan de zonen der reformatie hier te lande op Luther's vierde eeuwfeest aangeboden.* 2nd ed. Amsterdam: Höveker.

———. 1887. *Tweeërlei Vaderland: Ter inleiding van de zevende jaarvergadering der Vrije Universiteit.* Amsterdam: Wormser.

———. 1899. *Het Calvinisme: Zes Stone-lezingen in October 1898 te Princeton (N.-J.) gehouden.* Amsterdam: Höveker & Wormser.

———. 1905. *E Voto Dordraceno: Toelichting op den Heidelbergschen Catechismus II.* Amsterdam: Höveker & Wormser.

———. 1907. *Ons Program.* 5th ed. Amsterdam: Höveker & Wormser.

———. 1908-1909. *Encyclopaedie der Heilige Godgeleerdheid II, Algemeen deel.* 2nd ed. Kampen: Kok.

———. 1911-1912. *Pro Rege of het koningschap van Christus, I (Het koningschap van*

Christus in zijn hoogheid), II, III (Het koningschap van Christus in zijn werking). Kampen: Kok.

———. 1916. *Anti-Revolutionaire Staatkunde I (De beginselen).* Kampen: Kok.

———. 1931-1932. *De Gemeene Gratie I (Het geschiedkundig gedeelte), II (Het Leerstellig gedeelte), III (Het Praktisch gedeelte).* 3rd ed. Kampen: Kok.

Landman, G. M. 1995. *In de ruimte van de Naam: Liturgische grondwoorden in het Onderricht van Mozes en hun invloed op het Nieuwe Testament en de christelijke eredienst.* Zoetermeer: Boekencentrum.

Lumsdaine, David Halloran. 2009. *Evangelical Christianity and Democracy in Asia.* Oxford: Oxford University Press.

Mannion, Gerard. 2007. *Ecclesiology and Postmodernity: Questions for the Church in Our Time.* Collegeville: Michael Glazier.

Monsma, Stephen V., and J. Christopher Soper. 2008. *The Challenge of Pluralism: Church and State in Five Democracies.* 2nd ed. Lanham: Rowman & Littlefield Publishers.

Mouw, Richard J. 2011. *Abraham Kuyper: A Short and Personal Introduction.* Grand Rapids: Eerdmans.

Murphy, Nancey. 1996. *Beyond Liberalism and Fundamentalism: How Modern and Postmodern Philosophy Set the Theological Agenda.* New York: Bloomsbury T&T Clark.

Murray, Stuart. 2004. *Post-Christendom.* Carlisle: Paternoster.

Sanneh, Lamin, and Joel A. Carpenter, eds. 2005. *The Changing Face of Christianity: Africa, the West and the World.* Oxford: Oxford University Press.

Sengers, Erik. 2005. *The Dutch and Their Gods: Secularization and Transformation of Religions in the Netherlands since 1950.* Hilversum: Verloren.

Shanks, Andrew. 1995. *Civil Society, Civil Religion.* Oxford: Oxford University Press.

Sider, Ronald J. 2012. *Just Politics: A Guide for Christian Engagement.* 2nd ed. Grand Rapids: Brazos Press.

Smith, James K. A. 2009. *Desiring the Kingdom: Worship, Worldview, and Cultural Formation.* Grand Rapids: Baker Academic.

Trimp, C. 1983. *De gemeente en haar liturgie: Een leesboek voor kerkgangers.* Kampen: Van den Berg.

Van den Brink, G. 2004. *Een publieke zaak: Theologie tussen geloof en wetenschap.* Zoetermeer: Boekencentrum.

Van den Brink, G., and C. Van der Kooi. 2012. *Christelijke Dogmatiek.* Zoetermeer: Boekencentrum.

Volf, Miroslav. 1998. *After Our Likeness: The Church as Image of the Trinity.* Grand Rapids: Eerdmans.

Vree, Jasper, and Johan Zwaan. 2005a. *Abraham Kuyper's* Commentatio *(1860): The Young Kuyper about Calvin, à Lasco, and the Church.* Vol. I: *Introduction, Annotations, Bibliography, and Indices.* Leiden-Boston: Brill.

Vree, Jasper, and Johan Zwaan, eds. 2005b. *Abraham Kuyper's* Commentatio *(1860):*

The Young Kuyper about Calvin, à Lasco, and the Church. Vol. II: Commentatio. Leiden: Brill.

Wannenwetsch, Bernd. 2004. *Political Worship.* Oxford: Oxford University Press.

Wood, John Halsey, Jr. 2013. *Going Dutch in the Modern Age: Abraham Kuyper's Struggle for a Free Church in the Netherlands.* Oxford: Oxford University Press.

Wright, Nigel Goring. 2000. *Disavowing Constantine: Mission, Church and the Social Order in the Theologies of John Howard Yoder and Jürgen Moltmann; A Radical Baptist Perspective on Church, Society and State.* Carlisle: Paternoster.

Zijderveld, Anton C. 2000. *The Institutional Imperative: The Interface of Institutions and Networks.* Amsterdam: Amsterdam University Press.

Evolution as a Bone of Contention between Church and Academy: How Abraham Kuyper Can Help Us Bridge the Gap

Gijsbert van den Brink

Introduction

In November 2009, the Pew Research Center published a poll on "Public Opinion on Religion and Science in the United States."[1] It turned out that public attitudes towards contemporary science were mostly positive. There was one exception, however. A sharp and persistent clash between religion and science in the USA still centered on "evolution as the explanation of the origin and development of human life." According to a poll of scientists who are members of the American Association for the Advancement of Science (AAAS), the vast majority of scientists (97%) believe that life on earth has evolved over time (either due to natural processes only or guided by a supreme being); as to the general public, only 61% agree, whereas 31% of Americans directly reject evolution. When we look at evangelical Protestants among the general public, the figures are even more at variance: 35% agree that evolution has somehow occurred, whereas the majority (55%) deny this. So most evangelicals — as well as many members of mainline Protestant churches (26%) — are at odds with one of the most deeply embedded theories in contemporary science. Evolution, it seems, continues to be a sensitive bone of contention between church and academy.

1. See http://www.pewforum.org/2009/11/05/public-opinion-on-religion-and-science-in-the-united-states/. The poll was held in May/June 2009. For some more recent data (March/April 2013) on the general public's — not the scientists' — views on human evolution, see http://www.pewforum.org/2013/12/30/publics-views-on-human-evolution/ (last visited February 13, 2014). Although in this latter survey the general public is divided in slightly different categories than those used in 2009, it seems that no substantial changes were registered.

Irrespective of which side on the issue of evolution one takes, one can easily see that this is not a desirable situation. On the contrary, especially for those who want to prevent the chasm between the church and the academy from widening, this state of affairs is flatly disturbing. For on the one hand, it will make scientists suspicious of Christians and their faith, pushing them into the direction of other worldviews, among which naturalism takes pride of place. In this connection, it is a surprising outcome of the Pew research poll that even now only 8% of American scientists believe that evolution is a process guided by God or some other supreme being, whereas no less than 87% deem it entirely due to natural factors. Apparently, the tendency towards a naturalist interpretation of the data of evolutionary biology is very strong already. On the other hand, the clash on evolution will make many young and gifted Christians wary of specializing in one of the natural sciences and qualifying for a career as a scientist. Given this situation, it seems that Schleiermacher's concern that the tangle of history may unravel in such a way that Christianity becomes identified with barbarism and science with unbelief is still in place — perhaps even more so than it has ever been.[2] In the end, this is harmful both to the church and to the academy. To the church, because it may gradually become cut loose from one of the most influential cultural forces; and to the academy, because the advancement of science has always been enormously stimulated by the fact that its results could be shared by all kinds of people irrespective of their views of life.

Where should we look for help if we would like to remedy this unhelpful situation? When it comes to particular drawbacks of the evangelical American scene, Richard Mouw has proposed that we turn to Abraham Kuyper for guidance and correction.[3] So let us try to do this on the issue of evolution as well and see what happens. How did Abraham Kuyper in his day consider the issue of (human) evolution? Happily, we can answer this question, since in 1899 (one year after his famous Stone lectures in Princeton)[4] Kuyper devoted a rectorial address to the theme of evolution. An English translation of this address was published in 1996 in the *Calvin Theological Journal*.[5]

2. "Soll der Knoten der Geschichte so auseinandergehen, das Christentum mit der Barbarei und die Wissenschaft mit dem Unglauben?"; Schleiermacher 1990: 347, from the second letter to his pupil F. Lücke, 1829.

3. Cf., e.g., Mouw 2011.

4. Kuyper 1931; cf. Bratt 2013: 261-79.

5. Kuyper 1996: 11-50; subsequent quotes (including in-text quotations indicated by page numbers) refer to this translation. For the original Dutch text see Kuyper 1899. A slightly abridged English translation was published in Bratt 1998: 403-40.

Abraham Kuyper on Evolution

In an earlier rectorial address, *De verflauwing der grenzen* (1892), Kuyper had already mentioned evolution, and it is interesting to see from what perspective he evaluated it.[6] The speech consisted of a critical assessment of late nineteenth-century pantheism, and Kuyper saw evolutionary theory as pantheism's "legitimate daughter."[7] Although Kuyper had some sympathy for the religious origins of pantheism, in its post-Enlightenment form it had turned into a philosophical worldview which had pushed back its religious roots. Over against this worldview, which conflates the borderlines between God and world, it should be stated that there is "the most clearly defined boundary line" between God and the world.[8] Now evolutionary theory is a legitimate daughter of pantheism in this sense, that it denies any dividing lines whatsoever in all domains of human knowledge. So in Kuyper's eyes it even aggravates the problems of pantheism in that not only the boundary between God and the world is denied, but also all natural boundaries (such as those between plants and animals, animals and humans, etc.) within the created world.

Turning now to Kuyper's 1899 address, which was entirely devoted to the topic of evolution and which has been hailed as a brilliant and very well-informed speech,[9] we see that Kuyper continued to criticize evolution as an all-comprehensive worldview rather than a scientific theory. The opening sentence of the oration, which is famous for its rhetorical force, is instructive here: "Our nineteenth century is dying away under the hypnotic effect of the dogma of evolution." Indeed, Kuyper considered evolution as the indubitable dogma which enabled those who had turned away from Christ to erect their own worldview. Previously they had had to restrict themselves to the empirically observable, but now they were able to come up with a dogma that "could explain the entire cosmos by means of its monistic mechanics, including all life processes within that cosmos, the very earliest origins."[10] So they could now really put forward an alternative to Christianity as a worldview, by giving alternative answers to life's big and inescapable questions. Kuyper explicitly refers to

6. Kuyper 1892; for an English translation see "The Blurring of the Boundaries," in Bratt 1998: 363-402 (in-text quotations are from this translation).

7. Kuyper 1893: 762; the sentence is omitted from the later translation in Bratt 1998.

8. Kuyper, "Blurring of the Boundaries," in Bratt 1998: 374.

9. VU-biologist Jan Lever, in an interview with H. H. Kruyswijk, 29 April 2005; cf. Kruyswijk 2011: 48n107. See also Lever and Vlijm 1980: 269: "One can observe with astonishment and admiration that all kinds of claims he [Kuyper] makes are still relevant today."

10. Kuyper 1996: 12.

Herbert Spencer and especially Ernst Haeckel in order to substantiate his thesis that evolutionary theory is, in fact, an encompassing worldview, which even explains ethics (Spencer) and religion (Haeckel) from its monistic principle.[11]

It is quite understandable that throughout his oration Kuyper gives "an extensive and critical sketch" of evolutionary theory thus conceived.[12] Two things are pertinent in this connection, however. First of all, Kuyper concentrates his critique on the notion of teleology. The dogma of evolution "denies all pre-formation, that is, the governance of a plan over the budding of life" (16). "Anyone who still imagines that there can be any thought of purpose [*Zweck*], or of a compelling or guiding principle . . . simply does not know the dogma of evolution" (17). As Haeckel had said in plain terms: "The history of the world must be a physical-chemical process." So it is, first and foremost, the doctrine of divine providence which is at stake in evolutionary theory. It is, perhaps, especially as a Reformed theologian that Kuyper stresses this point from beginning to end, since arguably in classical Reformed theology the notions of God's eternal counsel and God's sovereignty over history are of paramount importance. Kuyper not only rejects this non-teleological worldview, but he also argues (and rightly so) that its correctness has not been demonstrated. "[I]t fancied that it had found the solution to the riddle of the universe, and in popular writings suggested that the architectonics of a 'cosmos without building plans' had been disclosed to us. Every satisfactory proof that the cosmos thus mechanistically formed itself is lacking, and the proof cannot be supplied, even experimentally, in step-by-step detail" (38).

Second, however, after having refuted evolutionary theory thus conceived for biological, aesthetical, ethical, and religious reasons, Kuyper rather unexpectedly shifts to another question, in a passage that has drawn a lot of attention from commentators:

> [T]he question whether religion, as such, permits a spontaneous unfolding of the species in organic life from the cytode or the nuclear cell, is an entirely different question. This question must be answered affirmatively, without reservation. We will not force our style upon the Chief Architect of the universe. If He is to be the Architect, not in name only but in reality, He will also be supreme in the choice of style. Therefore if it had pleased God not to create the species but to have one species emerge from another . . . creation would still be no less miraculous. However, this would never have been the

11. Kuyper 1996: 12.
12. Kuipers 2011: 310.

> evolution of Darwinism, for the pre-established purpose [*Zweck*] would then not have been banished but would have been all-controlling, and the world would not have constructed itself mechanistically, but God would have constructed it by the use of elements that He had himself prepared.[13]

One page further, Kuyper formulates the difference in a crystal clear way: "Evolutionistic creation presupposes a God who first prepares the plan and then omnipotently executes it. Darwinism teaches a mechanistic origin of things, which excludes all plan or specifications for purpose" (48). In lectures on the doctrine of creation that Kuyper gave during the same academic year (1899-1900), he made it clear that this "evolutionistic creation" should only be seen as a theoretical possibility. Not only do we lack any proof for the transition of one species to another, but also we have to acknowledge God-given boundaries between the inorganic and the organic, as well as between animals and humans.[14] As to his oration, Kuyper ends his speech in the same vein in which he started it, by firmly warning against evolution as "a newly conceived system, . . . a newly formed dogma, a newly emerged faith, which, embracing and dominating all of life, is diametrically opposed to the Christian faith, and can erect its temple only on the ruins of our Christian Confessions" (49-50).

The Reception of Kuyper's Speech on Evolution

Now what can we conclude from Kuyper's discussion of evolutionary theory as rendered above? Already during Kuyper's lifetime fierce debates emerged on the question whether Kuyper, while rejecting evolutionism as a worldview, had opened the gate for the reception of evolution more soberly conceived as a scientific theory — and these debates have continued until today. Indeed, it seemed to be the tenor of the unexpected interjection at the end of Kuyper's rectorial address that, when stripped of its ideological ramifications, evolutionary theory might be accepted. When in 1902 the Utrecht professor of biology Ambrosius Hubrecht judged in line with this that Kuyper's address had paved the way for his Reformed followers to accept evolutionary theory, however, this was vehemently denied in four anonymous articles in *De Heraut* (the Dutch neo-Calvinist weekly at the time); it was contended that Kuyper did not accept any aspect of the theory of evolution whatsoever.[15] As far as we know, Kuyper

13. Kuyper 1996: 47.
14. Cf. below, note 18.
15. See Kruyswijk 2011: 49 (also for further references).

himself never reacted in public to this exchange, which could be explained as support for the comments made in *De Heraut* (most probably by its editor-in-chief, W. Geesink). So it seems wrong to suggest, as Rob Visser has done, that Kuyper "was not very successful in persuading his co-religionists to revise their position."[16] Kuyper simply did not make an attempt to do so, or at least he did not continue his attempt.

Nevertheless, Visser rightly argues that Kuyper, along with Bavinck, "created a hermeneutical space to accommodate certain elements of Darwinism" (meaning by this especially the idea of species mutability).[17] For it should be noted that Kuyper's critical assessment of evolution and Darwinism was not based upon the exegesis of the first chapters of Genesis.[18] Although Kuyper had earlier explained these chapters using what might be called a literalistic reading,[19] in his address on evolution he refers to Genesis 1 only once, pointing out that this "Scriptural charter of creation eliminates rather than commends the *dramatic* entry of new beings."[20] God did not set down the various species on earth like pieces on a chessboard but *the earth brought forth* herbs, cattle, and other living beings (49).

So Kuyper seems to have changed his mind on the issue, although he did not repeat his new view later on. How can this be explained? The most reasonable explanation, it seems to me, is that the year before his evolution address Kuyper was in close contact with his fellow Calvinists in Princeton, especially with Benjamin Warfield (who had invited Kuyper to visit Princeton in order to receive an honorary doctorate and to give the Stone lectures just one year before his rectorial address on evolution). As is well known, Warfield had accepted evolutionary theory (though with certain qualifications), if not as a theory that was factually true, then in any case as a theory that, if true, could readily be accepted by Christians.[21] Now the young Dutch historian of science

16. Visser 2008: 295.

17. Visser 2008: 297; cf. 295.

18. Cf. Bratt's comment in Bratt 1998: 403: "He does not invoke literalistic readings of early Genesis, does not fantasize about Flood geology, and does not argue theology at all."

19. Kuyper 1891; on the background and non-authorized but still generally reliable status of these lecture-notes, see Kuipers 2011: 215-17. The notes stem from lectures Kuyper gave on the doctrine of creation during the academic year 1883-1884; Kuyper gave another series of lectures on the topic in 1899-1900, in which he now also discussed the theory of evolution (cf. Kuipers 2011: 326); student notes of this new series were included in Kuyper 1911.

20. Kuyper 1996: 49; the italicization of "dramatic" seems to stem from Kuyper (it is also in the Dutch original; see Kuyper 1899: 49.

21. Cf. Livingstone and Noll 2000: 283-304. The Livingstone/Noll thesis has been crit-

Ab Flipse has recently suggested that Kuyper's relatively open attitude toward evolution as a scientific theory in his 1899 rectorial address may be ascribed to this American contact. Warfield, in turn, explained Kuyper's tendency to consider evolution as a worldview rather than a scientific theory by pointing to "the neo-Calvinist view of science, which focused on presuppositions and principles, rather than on concrete results of scientific research."[22]

This being a plausible theory, we can summarize Kuyper's position on evolution as follows. First of all, Kuyper did not consider Darwinism as a scientific theory, but as the new driving force of a naturalistic worldview. In this respect, he agreed with Charles Hodge that "Darwinism is atheism."[23] Second, as far as he did consider *evolution* as a limited scientific theory on the origin of species, he was critical of it for factual reasons (like many of his contemporaries, and given the crisis of Darwinism around 1900 quite understandably so[24]), but did not reject it out of hand for religious reasons. Apparently, it was not the authority of Scripture that was at stake here according to Kuyper; and here, he seems to have followed Warfield. In fact, it has been demonstrated that it was only in the 1930s that a next generation of Dutch neo-Calvinists came to accept a creationist hermeneutics. Following the lead of Canadian fundamentalist George McCready Price, they consciously started to read the first chapters of Genesis from an anti-evolutionist perspective.[25]

Can Kuyper Help Us Bridge the Gap?

When evangelicals and other Christians resist evolutionary theory, they may have various reasons to do so, and it is important to investigate the nature of these reasons. According to some, of course, the authority of the Bible is at stake, for

---

icized and qualified by Zaspel 2010: 380-87; but even Zaspel has to admit that "there was an openness on Warfield's part to allowing evolution within a Christian framework" (381).

22. Flipse 2012: 112. See Warfield's review of Kuyper's "most instructive and inspiring address" (Warfield 1901: 296). Interestingly, the inverse hypothesis (attributing Warfield's hesitation on evolution to his knowledge of Kuyper's critical attitude) has been put forward by Peter S. Heslam; see Heslam 1998: 255-56. It seems to me that there need not be a contradiction here: both Flipse and Heslam may be right.

23. Cf. Hodge 1994.

24. Cf. Bratt 2013: 285-86; many scientific problems with Darwinism were resolved later on, esp. by the new theory of genetics and its synthesis with natural selection theory.

25. Hepp 1930: 181, 185-86; see also Aalders 1932: 296-97. See Flipse 2012: 124-26; Bratt 2013: 284 (Kuyper did not "quail at the prospect of a very old earth and resort to fantasies about Flood geology").

if we have to interpret the first chapters of Genesis in a non-literal way what else will follow? For others, it is the problem of evil that makes them wary of accepting evolutionary scenarios of the development of life. Surely there is a problem of evil anyhow, but it is aggravated by the enormous amount of suffering, waste of life, and extinction throughout the history of life on earth. Some Christians reject evolution because they just can't combine it with believing in the goodness of God. For still others, the issue of human uniqueness and (closely linked up with that) human dignity is decisive. If humans are just one more primate species, sharing their ancestors with the apes, how could they (and they alone of all species) bear the image of God? And then, of course, there are those who suspect that evolution destroys the whole Christian story of salvation by ruling out the possibility of a historical Adam and a historical Fall. As the old battle cry goes: "No Adam, no Fall; no Fall, no Atonement; no Atonement, no Savior."

All these fears and criticisms that people in the church have vis-à-vis evolution should be sincerely and seriously dealt with by Christian academics (and perhaps especially, or in any case also, by the theologians among them). It seems to me that, despite all current interest in issues of science and religion, far too few Christian academics are taking up this gauntlet. Perhaps especially in theological circles, where Ian G. Barbour's "independence model" of the relation between science and religion is still dominant, more attention and intellectual energy should be devoted to these questions.[26]

To what extent can Abraham Kuyper help us here? It is interesting that, as we saw, Kuyper in fact discerned only one major problem in evolutionary theory. Focusing on the extreme ideological interpretation of Darwin's theory given by Ernst Haeckel, Kuyper (like Hodge) judged that evolution ruled out any notion of divine guidance and providence. In his rectorial address on evolution, Kuyper made it clear time and again that this is the single big problem with evolution. Indeed, in Kuyper's day (like in ours) secular advocates of evolution presented evolutionary theory as an alternative worldview. It is not so strange, therefore, that Kuyper adopted their definition and targeted evolution as a "dogma," that is, as the guiding principle of an alternative worldview. However, as soon as Kuyper brought himself to distinguish evolution as a scientific theory from the ideological connotations which had accrued to the concept of evolution, he was far less critical. To be sure, he wasn't convinced of its truth, like Warfield seems to have been (at least during certain periods of his life). But neither did Kuyper put forward any principal religious or dogmatic objections against the possibility of a gradual development of life. The very

26. E.g. Barbour 1990: 3-30; cf. van den Brink 2009: 211-15, 224-33.

term he used approvingly in this connection, "evolutionistic creation," reminds us of what nowadays is called evolutionary creation (Denis Lamoureux)[27] or theistic evolution. So provided that there had been more evidence for the evolutionary development of life (such as we now have), Kuyper might have more seriously considered this stance. It was only after Kuyper that later neo-Calvinists began to close the door toward it in the slipstream of the budding American creationism. Thus, Kuyper can indeed help evangelicals and other Christians to bridge the current gap between church and academy on the issue of evolution, namely by pinpointing what should be seen as its biggest problem: its proneness to being abused for ideological purposes as an alternative worldview.

Let us finally consider to what extent this tendency is inherent in evolution as a scientific theory. For clearly, the Darwinian mechanism of natural selection on the basis of random mutations suffices to explain an amazingly great number of biological phenomena in immanent terms. No longer is there a need to see God at work behind the scenes of nature and history, as someone who governs and steers their course. In that sense, evolutionary theory came as liberation to all those who had their problems with the traditional doctrine of divine providence. True as this may be, however, evolution as a scientific theory does not *imply* that no God is involved in the way things go in the world. That conclusion just does not follow. The fact that we can no longer naively point to the natural world as indubitable evidence for the existence and providence of God (as William Paley famously thought — but he wasn't the only one), does not as such refute God's existence and providence. It only pushes us back to God's special revelation in Israel and Jesus Christ as by far the most important source of the Christian faith.[28]

Still, one might think that the sheer randomness of evolutionary processes rules out any divine involvement. However, it was already the Christian botanist Asa Gray, a good friend of Darwin and the first propagator of his views in the United States, who pointed out that in his providential guidance of the world God can have built-in random processes. The fact that all kinds of mutations strike *us* as completely random and arbitrary does not mean that they necessarily are unguided or unintended from God's point of view.[29] Already in 1884 Anglican theologian Frederick Temple put it quite well when he suggested that rather than being demeaning to God, evolutionary processes might just

27. Lamoureux 2008.

28. See art. 2 of the *Belgic Confession* (1561), and cf. van den Brink 2011: 273-92.

29. See for a convincing argument here Plantinga 2011: xii, 39, 308-9.

as well heighten our awe for God's power and wisdom, since apparently God was not only able to make things, but also, and more ingeniously, to "make things make themselves."

Conclusion

In sum, then, it is important for contemporary evangelical Christians to see what Kuyper saw, viz. that creation and evolution are complementary rather than competing terms. Evolutionary theory tells us nothing about how it all started (as Darwin was well aware of), but only about how life on earth evolved. Conversely, creation doesn't tell us how living beings on earth developed but only how it all started in the first place (according to Christians and other theists). So, strictly speaking, there is no contradiction here. It is as Kuyper already argued in his rectorial address: the world isn't less miraculous if God made it by using evolutionary processes. Now, admittedly, this crucial insight might be found more clearly and consistently in Warfield than in Kuyper, so American evangelicals might just as well turn to "their own" Warfield for help in facing the current gap between the academy and the church on evolution. But since prophets usually are not honored in their home countries, Kuyper may be important as well here, especially to those who are already impressed by Kuyper's Christian thinking for other reasons.[30]

REFERENCES

Aalders, G. Ch. 1932. *De Goddelijke openbaring in de eerste drie hoofdstukken van Genesis.* Kampen: J. H. Kok.

Barbour, Ian G. 1990. *Religion in an Age of Science.* London: SCM Press.

Bratt, James D., ed. 1998. *Abraham Kuyper: A Centennial Reader.* Grand Rapids: Eerdmans.

———. 2013. *Abraham Kuyper: Modern Calvinist, Christian Democrat.* Grand Rapids: Eerdmans.

Flipse, Abraham C. 2012. "The Origins of Creationism in the Netherlands: The Evolution Debate among Twentieth-Century Dutch Neo-Calvinists." *Church History* 81: 104-47.

30. I am grateful to Abraham C. Flipse (VU University), Sam De Groot (Dordt College), as well as to the audience of the 2013 Kuyper Conference at Princeton Theological Seminary for their helpful comments on an earlier draft of this paper.

Hepp, Valentine. 1930. *Calvinism and the Philosophy of Nature: The Stone Lectures Delivered at Princeton in 1930*. Grand Rapids: Eerdmans.

Heslam, Peter S. 1998. *Creating a Christian Worldview: Abraham Kuyper's Lectures on Calvinism*. Grand Rapids: Eerdmans.

Hodge, Charles. 1994 (1874). *What Is Darwinism? and Other Writings on Science and Religion*, ed. and introduced by Mark A. Noll. Grand Rapids: Baker Book House.

Kruyswijk, H. H. 2011. *Baas in eigen Boek? Evolutietheorie en Schriftgezag bij de Gereformeerde Kerken in Nederland (1881-1981)*. Hilversum: Uitgeverij Verloren.

Kuipers, Tjitze. 2011. *Abraham Kuyper: An Annotated Bibliography, 1857-2010*. Leiden: Brill.

Kuyper, Abraham. 1891. *Locus de Creatione: College-dictaat van onderscheidene studenten*. Amsterdam: J. A. Wormser.

———. 1892. *De verflauwing der grenzen: Rede bij de overdracht van het rectoraat aan de Vrije Universiteit op 20 october 1892*. Amsterdam: J. A. Wormser.

———. 1893. "Pantheism's Destruction of Boundaries — Part 2." *The Methodist Review* 75: 762-78.

———. 1899. *Evolutie: Rede bij de overdracht van het rectoraat aan de Vrije Universiteit op 20 october 1899 gehouden*. Amsterdam: Höveker & Wormser.

———. 1911. *Dictaten dogmatiek van Dr. Abraham Kuyper. II Locus de Sacra Scriptura, Creatione, Creaturis*. Kampen: J. H. Kok.

———. 1931 (1899). *Lectures on Calvinism*. Grand Rapids: Eerdmans.

———. 1996. "Evolution." *Calvin Theological Journal* 31: 11-50.

Lamoureux, Denis. 2008. *Evolutionary Creation: A Christian Approach to Evolution*. Eugene: Wipf & Stock.

Lever, J., and L. Vlijm. 1980. "Biologie." In *Wetenschap en rekenschap 1880-1980: Een eeuw wetenschapsbeoefening en wetenschapsbeschouwing aan de Vrije Universiteit*, ed. M. van Os and W. J. Wierenga, pp. 261-71. Kampen: J. H. Kok.

Livingstone, David L., and Mark A. Noll. 2000. "B. B. Warfield (1851-1921): A Biblical Inerrantist as Evolutionist." *Isis* 9: 283-304.

Mouw, Richard J. 2011. *Abraham Kuyper: A Short and Personal Introduction*. Grand Rapids: Eerdmans.

Plantinga, Alvin. 2011. *Where the Conflict Really Lies: Science, Religion, and Naturalism*. Oxford: Oxford University Press.

Schleiermacher, Friedrich. 1990. *Theologisch-dogmatische Abhandlungen und Gelegenheitsschriften*. Kritische Gesamtausgabe, Schriften und Entwürfe Bd. 10. Berlin: Walter de Gruyter.

Van den Brink, Gijsbert. 2009. *Philosophy of Science for Theologians: An Introduction*. Frankfurt am Main: Peter Lang.

———. 2011. "A Most Elegant Book: The Natural World in Article 2 of the *Belgic Confession*." *Westminster Theological Journal* 73: 273-92.

Visser, Rob P. W. 2008. "Dutch Calvinists and Darwinism, 1900-1960." In *Nature and*

Scripture in the Abrahamic Religions, Vol. 2: *1700-Present*, ed. Jitse M. van der Meer and Scott Mandelbrote, pp. 293-315. Leiden: Brill.

Warfield, B. B. 1901. "Review of Abraham Kuyper, Evolutie: Rede bij de overdracht van het rectoraat aan de Vrije Universiteit op 20 October, 1899." *The Presbyterian and Reformed Review* 12: 296.

Zaspel, Fred G. 2010. *The Theology of B. B. Warfield: A Systematic Summary*. Wheaton: Crossway.

A Queen without a Throne? Harnack, Schlatter, and Kuyper on Theology in the University

Michael Bräutigam

Theology today is in a crisis. Right at the beginning, when the Western universities were born almost a thousand years ago, theology was the queen of sciences. Things changed, however, with the Enlightenment, when human reason stole theology's crown. And if theology was to remain at the university, it would have to pursue its task within the limits of pure reason. Today, theology finds itself facing an identity crisis. Who are theologians? And what are they doing? Are they historians with a special focus on Christian church history? Are they analytical philosophers of religion? Or are they simply linguists with a special focus on the Greek and Hebrew languages? Theology is in an identity crisis and common sense tells us that having a crisis makes one vulnerable. In the academy, theology is thus increasingly sidelined and marginalized.[1] This is reflected by the global phenomenon where the theological faculty is simply swallowed by the — perhaps more pluralist? — religious studies department; Oxford University's theological faculty, for instance, was recently renamed the "faculty of theology and religion."[2] This development could be the end of

1. This is also reflected in the political pressure put on the theological faculties. In 2008, the German government's science counsel *(Wissenschaftsrat)* asked the Protestant theological faculties to explain "which historical and/or systematic reasons would speak for or against the establishment of theology at the university." See Günther Thomas, "Die Aufgabe der Evangelischen Theologie im Ensemble universitärer Religionsforschung: Eine Zumutung," *Zeitschrift für dialektische Theologie* 28, no. 2 (2012): 4-28.

2. A couple of years ago, the theological college and religious studies department of Queen's University in Kingston, Ontario, Canada was renamed the "School of Religious Studies." On the website, the renaming is advertised under the following heading: "School of Re-

the theological faculty as we know it. But it does not have to be that way. In early twentieth-century Germany, the Protestant faculties faced quite a similar threat and, thanks to Protestant theologian Adolf von Harnack, they survived. Perhaps it might be worthwhile considering Harnack's arguments from the past, analyzing whether one can apply some of those to our situation today.

In this short essay, I will thus make the — humble — attempt to argue for theology as a *primus inter pares,* for theology as *Wissenschaft* that assesses and makes propositional truth claims, promotes communication within the university, and thus brings the postmodern *multi*versity back to a proper *uni*versity. To support the argument I intend to introduce authorities in this matter. While those experts might be figures from the past, the author is convinced that some of their ideas will provide a vital stimulus for our public discourse today. More precisely, this brief study offers a comparison of three speeches delivered by the already mentioned Adolf von Harnack (1851-1930), the Swiss Reformed theologian Adolf Schlatter (1852-1938), and the Dutch neo-Calvinist Abraham Kuyper (1837-1920). In the following first part we shall analyze these three influential speeches, while examining, second, in which ways they could help us today to define the present (and future) role of Christian theology at the university.

Adolf von Harnack on "The Task of the Theological Faculties"

In the summer of 1901, Adolf von Harnack gave the rectorial address at the University of Berlin, where he had been serving as professor of church history for some time.[3] At the dawn of a new century, Harnack offers a substantial response to critical voices who demanded the renaming of the "Faculty for Christian Theology" as a "Faculty for General Science of Reli-

---

ligion renamed: We're not here to promote faith, but rather to promote the understanding of religion as a human phenomenon." http://queensjournal.ca/story/2010-03-26/news/school-religion-renamed/ (accessed April 11, 2013).

3. Adolf von Harnack lectured as associate professor *(ausserordentliche Professur)* at his alma mater in Leipzig (1875-78); he then moved to Giessen where he served as professor of church history (1879-86), followed then by Marburg (1886-88), and finally Berlin (1888-21). Harnack was a member of the Academy of Sciences, he served as the editor of the *Theologische Literaturzeitung,* he was the Rector of the University of Berlin, the Director of the Royal Library, and the first president of the Kaiser-Wilhelm Foundation (today: Max-Planck-Gesellschaft). On Harnack's life and work see the compendium edited by Kurt Nowak and Otto Gerhard Oexle, *Adolf von Harnack: Theologe, Historiker, Wissenschaftspolitiker Christentum, Wissenschaft und Gesellschaft* (Göttingen: Vandenhoeck & Ruprecht, 2001).

gion and History of Religion" *(Fakultät für allgemeine Religionsgeschichte).*[4] Only in this way, Harnack's opponents, such as Paul de Lagarde (1827-91) of Göttingen and Franz Overbeck (1837-1905) of Basle, argued, would the faculty be more inclusive, more pluralistic, and thereby meeting the "modern" demands of science, of *Wissenschaftlichkeit.*[5] At this point, one wonders why this plea could have presented a problem for Harnack, who fought so enthusiastically for theology as a *Wissenschaft?*[6] In what follows, we shall take a closer look at Harnack's speech on "The Task of the Theological Faculties and the General History of Religion" in order to carve out his position in more detail.

Harnack opens his speech by introducing the arguments of his opponents who were arguing for the re-baptism of the theological faculty.[7] What kind of arguments, Harnack asks, could possibly speak for such a move? First, he concedes, abstract theoretical considerations might favor this decision. Religion, Harnack says, is an elementary part of humanity, and it is thus indeed defensible not to reduce one's observations to just one single religion.[8] Second, still playing devil's advocate, Harnack admits that religion can only be examined with the historical method (and this Harnack regards as consensus); and as the method itself must not be restricted in any way, for the sake of pure science, the scope must thus be extended to other religions as well.[9] Third, Harnack grants that ecclesial reasons, too, might provide arguments for a renaming of the theological faculties. In the wake of the late nineteenth- and early twentieth-century European imperialism, as Christian missionaries were sent to the four corners of the earth, Harnack, infused by the *Zeitgeist* of imperialistic Culture Protestantism, deems it indeed necessary to "carefully examine the religions of the foreign peoples" in

4. Harnack, "Die Aufgabe der theologischen Fakultäten und die allgemeine Religionsgeschichte nebst einem Nachwort," in *Reden und Aufsätze II/1* (Gießen: J. Ricker'sche Verlagsbuchhandlung, 1904), 164. Unless otherwise indicated, all translations are my own.

5. For the overall context of the struggle see Thomas A. Howard, *Protestant Theology and the Making of the Modern German University* (Oxford: Oxford University Press, 2006), 380-91.

6. See Harnack, "Fünfzehn Fragen an die Verächter der wissenschaftlichen Theologie unter den Theologen (1923)," in *Adolf von Harnack als Zeitgenosse: Reden und Schriften aus den Jahren des Kaiserreichs und der Weimarer Republik,* ed. Kurt Nowak, vol. 1 (Berlin: De Gruyter, 1996), 875-79.

7. Harnack, "Aufgabe der theologischen Fakultäten," 164.

8. Harnack, "Aufgabe der theologischen Fakultäten," 164-65.

9. According to Harnack, the one scientific historical-critical method fits all. There is not a special "Christian" method to investigate Christianity and another method to analyze another religion. See Harnack, "Aufgabe der theologischen Fakultäten," 165-66.

order to be able to preach the gospel to them more clearly.[10] Having said that, Harnack finds, even so, none of these reasons convincing enough to allow a renaming of the theological faculties to "Faculties for a General History of Religion." Harnack highlights three key arguments why he emphatically decides against this proposal.

First of all, Harnack claims that a universal treatment of all kinds of religions under the one roof of one faculty of religion would necessarily end up in an "unhealthy dilettantism" *(heillosen Dilettantismus)*.[11] To Harnack's mind, a thorough understanding of a religion inevitably involves a careful analysis of the religion's specific linguistic and socio-political as well as historical context. This is simply due to the fact that "in the history of linguistics is mirrored the history of religion."[12] This task could perhaps, Harnack admits, be mastered to a certain degree with a view to one single religion, such as Christianity. Yet a broader scope would ask too much of the soon to be overburdened faculty of religion and would, sooner or later, lead to a collapse of the quality of theological research. Second, Harnack explains, unmistakably building on Friedrich Schleiermacher, that the sheer scope and universality of Christianity clearly justifies a distinct treatment within the walls of a Christian theological faculty, where all the research energy is focused on this one "superior" religion.[13] Buoyed by a proud and overly optimistic pre–World War I outlook, Harnack exclaims:

> Whoever does not know this religion [i.e., Christianity], knows no religion at all, and whoever knows it, along with its history, knows all [religions]. . . . What is the significance of Homer, what are the Vedas, what is the Koran next to the Bible?[14]

Moreover, reminiscent of Schleiermacher, Harnack is also convinced that one finds in Christianity a lived "piety" *(Frömmigkeit)* that is unparalleled in the

10. Harnack, "Aufgabe der theologischen Fakultäten," 166.

11. Harnack, "Aufgabe der theologischen Fakultäten," 167.

12. Harnack, "Aufgabe der theologischen Fakultäten," 167.

13. Friedrich Schleiermacher (1768-1834), who co-founded this first modern university in the West together with Wilhelm von Humboldt (1769-1859) in 1809 in the first place, argued that of all the monotheistic religions, Christianity is "in fact the quintessential among the most developed forms of religion" *(in der That die vollkommenste unter den am meisten entwikkelten Religionsformen)*. Schleiermacher, *Der christliche Glaube nach den Grundsätzen der evangelischen Kirche im Zusammenhange dargestellt: 2. Auflage (1830/31) — Erster und zweiter Band*, ed. Rolf Schäfer (Berlin: Walter de Gruyter, 2008), §8, I:71.

14. Harnack, "Aufgabe der theologischen Fakultäten," 168.

world and which thus deserves special treatment.[15] Harnack offers a third reason why he thinks the status quo of the theological faculties should be maintained. Again echoing Schleiermacher, Harnack argues that Christianity is the religion par excellence, which justifies its exclusivity at the university. "We wish," Harnack expresses, "that the theological faculties remain [exclusively] to investigate the Christian religion, as Christianity is in its purest form not a religion among others, but *the* religion."[16] Why is that the case? At this point Harnack reveals, perhaps surprising to many a conservative contemporary, a distinctly Christocentric focus. Christianity is supreme simply because Jesus Christ is not "a master among others, but *the* master."[17] Jesus Christ is and should be, in Harnack's view, *the* "center" *(Mittelpunkt)* of every study at the theological faculty.[18] For this reason, Christian theology deserves a "special place" *(besonderen Platz)* within the university, right among the sciences, as a distinct theological faculty, and not to be degraded to a general *Religionswissenschaft* to be subsumed under too broad a roof.[19]

In addition to the reasons already outlined, Harnack also argues strongly for theology's freedom in general. That is, Harnack is quick to add that theology must remain independent from any interference by the church. Theology, as a proper member of the faculty of sciences, possesses the same rights as every other science, namely the right of freedom, freedom in particular from ecclesial ties and tutelage.[20] "In pursuing our historical work," Harnack claims, "we cannot and we must not consider the teachings and the needs of the church."[21] This clearly shows how far Harnack was removed from the position of the traditional and confessional churches by then; and with a pinch of mischievous condescension Harnack admits that theology is, of course, still prepared to offer advice and assistance to the church (all the while forgetting that theology's main purpose within the Prussian university system was still the education of the future clergy).[22] Be that

15. In addition, Harnack contends, again, basically reiterating Schleiermacher, that the lived "piety" *(Frömmigkeit)* that is to be found in the Christian religion, for example "in a puritan Christian in America," is a type of "Christian piety" unparalleled in either Buddhism or Islam. Harnack, "Aufgabe der theologischen Fakultäten," 172. Schleiermacher speaks of a kind of "teleological piety" *(teleologische Frömmigkeit)* which finds its highest expression in Christianity. *Der Christliche Glaube,* §9, I:77, 80.

16. Harnack, "Aufgabe der theologischen Fakultäten," 172 (emphasis added).

17. Harnack, "Aufgabe der theologischen Fakultäten," 172 (emphasis added).

18. Harnack, "Aufgabe der theologischen Fakultäten," 173.

19. Harnack, "Aufgabe der theologischen Fakultäten," 173.

20. Harnack, "Aufgabe der theologischen Fakultäten," 175, 177.

21. Harnack, "Aufgabe der theologischen Fakultäten," 176.

22. Harnack, "Aufgabe der theologischen Fakultäten," 176.

as it may, judged from today's perspective, Harnack won the argument; in other words, his speech was the deathblow to the growing surge of *Religionswissenschaft* in German universities, and he successfully secured the place of theology within the German faculty until now.[23]

Having briefly outlined Harnack's position, we shall now move to Adolf Schlatter, his contemporary and colleague who lectured alongside Harnack in Berlin between 1893 and 1898. As a matter of fact, Harnack was indirectly responsible for Schlatter's call to Berlin. Having published a critical view on the Apostles' Creed *(Apostolikum)* in 1892, Harnack was faced with disciplinary action.[24] In order to appease the outraged ecclesial camp, the Prussian ministry of culture (literally the "ministry of the cult" — the *Kultusministerium* — still the commonly used term today) decided to install a chair of systematic theology at the University of Berlin that would support the church's position and thus counterbalance Harnack. This so-called "punitive professorship" *(Strafprofessur)* was awarded to none other than Adolf Schlatter, and, what came as a surprise to many, Harnack and Schlatter became against all the odds something like friends, which, of course, does not mean that they agreed on all theological matters.[25]

Adolf Schlatter laid out his position on theology's role within the university in a speech delivered in the same year as Harnack's, in 1901. At that time, Schlatter had already turned his back on Berlin. Having moved to Swabia a

23. Thomas A. Howard writes: "Although one cannot attribute the weakened position of *Religionswissenschaft* in Germany in the early twentieth century solely to Harnack's influential address, a number of his contemporaries and later commentators interpreted this to be the case, and I am inclined to think there is merit in this view." *Protestant Theology and the Making of the Modern German University,* 394.

24. With his critical stance towards the *Apostolikum,* Harnack had maneuvered himself into a precarious situation. The Evangelical-Lutheran Conference of September 20, 1892, formulated an official complaint on whose basis emperor Wilhelm II asked for an immediate report *(Immediatbericht)* on Harnack. Prussian culture minister Julius R. Bosse (1832-1901) was able to aid Harnack in this predicament and, in order to appease the ecclesial camp, suggested the installation of a chair for systematic theology at the University of Berlin that would support the church position. This suggestion was endorsed by Wilhelm II as the so-called "punitive professorship" *(Strafprofessur)* against Harnack which was finally awarded to Schlatter. For a summary of the *Apostolikumsstreit* see Karl Neufeld, *Adolf Harnacks Konflikt mit der Kirche: Weg-Stationen zum "Wesen des Christentums"* (Innsbruck: Tyrolia, 1979), 114-32.

25. As Schlatter was awarded his chair as a penal professorship against Harnack, one would expect a chilly reception in Berlin. Surprisingly, at least to Schlatter, Harnack had already written a welcoming letter a few months earlier, in March 1893, whose friendly tone would not only be reciprocated by Schlatter but would also mark their positive future etiquette despite theological disagreement.

few years earlier, Schlatter was now professor of systematic theology and New Testament in Tübingen.[26]

Adolf Schlatter on "Today's Religious Task of the Universities"

"What Is Today's Religious Task of the Universities?" *(Was ist heute die religiöse Aufgabe der Universitäten?);* this is the question Schlatter addresses in his speech at the University of Tübingen.[27] One instantly notices the broader scope of Schlatter's paper. In contrast to Harnack, Schlatter does not intend to focus solely on the theological faculty. Instead, pursuing a holistic perspective, he argues for a distinct religious, ethical imperative that is intrinsic not only to theology, but applies to all the sciences at the university. This deserves a closer examination.

The main problem Schlatter identified was the increasing diversity and the lack of unity within the university. The university, as he saw it, was suffering from an internal conflict. Faculties were approached with a cacophony of demands and wishes. In terms of the theological faculty, for instance, the church wanted it to represent their confessional position whereas more liberal streams argued for a pursuit of Idealism.[28] As highlighted earlier, Schlatter himself became the pawn in the power game between church politicians and the Prussian ministry of culture. Schlatter thus attempted to find a common denominator, an overarching definition of the university's ethical task. What was it that really made the university a *uni*-versity and not a *di*-versity or *multi*-versity? This is Schlatter's suggestion as he put it in his speech: "Everything that creates understanding [*Verständnis*]," he argues, "and keeps the [flow of] communication going, has therefore immediate religious value."[29] Following Schlatter, the religious-ethical task of the university is thus twofold: first, it is to "create understanding" and, second, it needs to "keep the flow of communication going." In what follows we shall briefly consider these two aspects.

26. For a short introduction to Schlatter's life and theology see Peter Stuhlmacher's essay in Martin Greschat, ed., *Theologen des Protestantismus im 19. und 20. Jahrhundert II* (Stuttgart: Kohlhammer, 1978), 219-40. Robert Yarbrough has translated Werner Neuer's short biography, *Adolf Schlatter: A Biography of Germany's Premier Biblical Theologian* (Grand Rapids: Baker Books, 1995). Werner Neuer's magisterial Schlatter biography is, unfortunately, still untranslated, *Adolf Schlatter: Ein Leben für Theologie und Kirche* (Stuttgart: Calwer Verlag, 1996).

27. Schlatter, "Was ist heute die religiöse Aufgabe der Universitäten?," *Beiträge zur Förderung Christlicher Theologie* 5, no. 4 (1901): 61-79.

28. Schlatter, "Religiöse Aufgabe der Universitäten," 67.

29. Schlatter, "Religiöse Aufgabe der Universitäten," 71.

Primarily, then, the university's religious-ethical value consists in "creating understanding." Schlatter makes the case that the university is not a self-sufficient, isolated island. On the contrary: the university is organically integrated within the socio-cultural landscape;[30] and all faculties, whatever their subject might be, influence society and culture in a distinct ethical way.[31] In Schlatter's view, "the work of the universities influences the [society's] present religious condition."[32] It so does in particular as it pursues the quest for truth, creating understanding and accumulating knowledge. Schlatter is adamant that "[e]very thought [at the university] is guided by the canon of truth."[33] And in its pursuit of truth, the university must ensure impartiality and openness to all different kinds of mindsets and movements.[34] The chairs at the university, Schlatter says, "must accommodate all intellectual movements with a maximum of courtesy."[35] That is, in order to fulfill the ethical task of creating knowledge, the university must ensure academic freedom. This is how he puts it in his speech:

> The religious dignity of our profession is bound . . . to the canon of truthfulness. As the obedient ones who are bound to this demand we are the freest of the free, in the full possession of our academic freedom Exercising this obedience correctly and keeping this bondage unharmed is immanent to the university's task and its service to God [*Gottesdienst*].[36]

As he argues for a maximum of freedom of the scientific endeavor, Schlatter is, much like Harnack as noted earlier, critical of any interference from the outside.[37] The ethical *leitmotif* of the university is thus the "creation of under-

30. Schlatter, "Religiöse Aufgabe der Universitäten," 64.

31. Schlatter, "Religiöse Aufgabe der Universitäten," 66.

32. Schlatter, "Religiöse Aufgabe der Universitäten," 66.

33. Schlatter, "Religiöse Aufgabe der Universitäten," 71.

34. This explains why for Schlatter confessional allegiance was never pivotal although he was clearly rooted in the Reformed faith. Schlatter kept a confessional openness that did not make his life easier, as the Liberals regarded him as an orthodox sheep in wolf's clothing, and the conservative Lutherans regarded him as a liberal wolf in an orthodox sheepskin. The decisive factor for Schlatter then was not church confession or philosophical allegiance, but faithfulness to one's profession in being rigorously dedicated to the quest for truth through careful empirical observation of the facts, the close observation of the "objectively given facts" *(objektiv gegebene Thatbestand),* as he put it. Schlatter, "Religiöse Aufgabe der Universitäten," 72n1. In this context, see also my contribution, "Seeing, Thinking, and Living: Adolf Schlatter on Theology at the University," *Scottish Bulletin of Evangelical Theology* 30, no. 2 (2012): 177-88.

35. Schlatter, "Religiöse Aufgabe der Universitäten," 74.

36. Schlatter, "Religiöse Aufgabe der Universitäten," 77.

37. "Such a protection [through the state]," Schlatter notes, "is unworthy and works

standing" through the pursuit of truth; and in this pursuit, the university is endowed with full academic freedom as it serves society. Moreover, and this is significant for our observations, Schlatter seems to say here that the university's task of pursuing truth in full academic freedom has in itself religious-ethical value as it represents an act of worship *(Gottesdienst)*. The medical researcher who develops a new treatment thus creates knowledge not only to the good of humankind, but she thereby also glorifies God — as does the engineer who develops a safer car or the lawyer who secures justice. Schlatter makes a case for the ethical dignity of all areas of research at the university.

However, and this is the second point, in order to fulfill this role properly, scholars must ensure that the flow of communication is guaranteed, both within the university and with the outside. On the one hand, this means that the academic needs to talk to her colleagues in other fields of interest. Schlatter himself, always suspicious of professional hermits, practiced collegial exchange throughout his career, and he showed interest in other areas than "merely" theology, publishing works in the fields of linguistics, archeology, ethics, and philosophy. On the other hand, Schlatter underlines that the university's ethical role is only then fully carried out when the "flow of communication" happens also between the university and society. The scholar is thus never to retreat to a cozy niche in the ivory tower but to remain actively in touch with society, culture, and the overall *Zeitgeist*. Again, Schlatter practiced what he preached; he showed in his own life what a scholar's active engagement in society can look like, and ten years after this address in Tübingen, Schlatter's service to the university, to the church, and to society as a whole was officially recognized when the King of Württemberg awarded Schlatter the *Order of the Crown* and ennobled him (of which Schlatter, however, rarely made use).[38] The ethical role of the university, the free "creation of understanding," is in Schlatter's view thus only then fully achieved when the transfer of knowledge happens not only internally but also externally; only in this way does the university serve humanity to the glory of God.

Abraham Kuyper: Sphere Sovereignty

We shall now move both on the map (westward, to the Netherlands) and in time (backward, to the year 1880). Abraham Kuyper faced similar challenges

---

detrimental towards the fulfillment of its task." Schlatter, "Religiöse Aufgabe der Universitäten," 74.

38. See Neuer, *Adolf Schlatter*, 460.

to Harnack in terms of a restructuring of the theological faculty.[39] The Higher Education Act of 1876 legally required Dutch universities to replace theology with religious studies, although the title "theology" was retained.[40] In contrast to Harnack, however, who remained at the university, fighting the fight from within as it were, Kuyper chose a different strategy. The Dutch theologian saw fit to establish a distinct Christian university with a theological faculty, in order to counterbalance the assault on the theological faculty. On October 20, 1880, Abraham Kuyper spoke at the inauguration of the Free University of Amsterdam *(Vrije Universiteit).* The title of this landmark speech is "Sphere Sovereignty." "Sphere sovereignty," according to Kuyper, must be the "hallmark" of this newly established university.[41] What is sphere sovereignty and what does it have to do with the university?

For Kuyper, God is the ultimate Sovereign who possesses absolute sovereignty.[42] God delegates his sovereign authority to humanity which is thus endowed with a derived sovereignty. Kuyper assumes several different sovereign spheres, such as social and ecclesial life, and science, for instance. The state has a "special sphere of authority" as it ensures the "sound mutual interaction" among the various spheres.[43] That is, the state, Kuyper clarifies, must never impose its own standards to the other spheres, but must "see that the wheels operate as intended."[44] In other words, the state as the "sphere of spheres" merely fixes the "boundaries" of the other spheres by law.[45] And as the spheres interact with one another, the "multifaceted multiformity of human life" unfolds.[46] Clearly, the trademark of the university in Kuyper's view is sphere sovereignty. Kuyper is emphatic that "scholarship remains 'Sovereign in its own sphere' and does not degenerate under the guardianship of Church or State."[47] Anything else would be in fact a sinful

39. On Abraham Kuyper, see the new biography by James D. Bratt, *Abraham Kuyper: Modern Calvinist, Christian Democrat* (Grand Rapids: Eerdmans, 2013).

40. See James Eglinton and Michael Bräutigam, "Scientific Theology? Herman Bavinck and Adolf Schlatter on the Place of Theology in the University," *Journal of Reformed Theology* 7 (2013): 39-43.

41. Kuyper, *Souvereiniteit in eigen kring* (Amsterdam: J. H. Kruyt, 1880); we use the English translation: "Sphere Sovereignty," in *Abraham Kuyper: A Centennial Reader,* ed. James D. Bratt (Grand Rapids: Eerdmans, 1998), 464.

42. Kuyper, "Sphere Sovereignty," 466.

43. Kuyper, "Sphere Sovereignty," 468.

44. Kuyper, "Sphere Sovereignty," 468.

45. Kuyper, "Sphere Sovereignty," 472.

46. Kuyper, "Sphere Sovereignty," 467-68.

47. Kuyper, "Sphere Sovereignty," 476.

move, he adds;[48] Richard J. Mouw even speaks in that respect of "Kuyper's antiecclesiasticist impulse."[49] While neither Schlatter nor Harnack referred to Kuyper's concept of sphere sovereignty, one detects here a general overlap of their strong emphasis on the freedom and independence of the academy from any outside interference.

In his speech, Kuyper also tackles the clash of worldviews in the academy, what he calls a "conflict of principles."[50] He sees a wide gulf between what he later calls in his Princeton Stone Lectures the "Christian scholars" *(Abnormalists)* and the "atheist scholars" *(Normalists).*[51] This "battle of ideas," Kuyper says, "is possible and necessary . . . but never over anything but starting point and direction."[52] While all three theologians surely agreed on the reality of this underlying battle of worldviews, they decided to contend from different positions. Kuyper established the Free University as an answer to state universities, which he regarded as being infested with the "normalist" mindset of modernism and liberalism. The Free University should function as a sovereign entity, representing the biblical worldview on the marketplace of intellectual movements. In reality things became rather difficult for Kuyper. On the one hand, the Dutch Reformed Church hesitated to welcome ministers educated at the Free University; and on the other hand, the state at first refused to accredit the degrees obtained by the students, which meant that they had to pass qualifying examinations twice.[53] In contrast to Kuyper, Harnack and Schlatter decided not to leave the battlefield of the state university to fight from the fortress of their own Christian university or from the stronghold of an independent biblical seminary. And even today, many a theologian is faced with the question of choosing a strategic position in face of the ongoing clash of worldviews, either fighting from within a pluralist (post)modern university or rather from an independent theological seminary.

Having considered some basic viewpoints of these significant figures of the past, we are now in a position to reflect on a vision for theology today, in relation to the academy, the church, and society. The following section discusses some central suggestions based on our considerations so far.

48. Kuyper, "Sphere Sovereignty," 476.

49. Mouw, "The Seminary, the Church, and the Academy," 459.

50. Kuyper, "Sphere Sovereignty," 487.

51. Kuyper, *Lectures on Calvinism* (Grand Rapids: Eerdmans, 1931), 136-37.

52. Kuyper, "Sphere Sovereignty," 486.

53. Bratt, *Abraham Kuyper: Modern Calvinist, Christian Democrat*, 123.

Toward a Vision for Today — Some Suggestions

Adolf Harnack, Adolf Schlatter, and Abraham Kuyper were all faced with the threat of a marginalization of theology in the academy. The theologian, as Kuyper put it, "has been forced out of the official house, [and] is now obliged to look for a place where he may lay down his head."[54] In this sense, times have not really changed. Today, one is often confronted with the claim that theology has no real place in the academy; it is deemed less precise and less professional than the natural sciences and it is being portrayed as irrational and irrelevant as it only presents grand narratives of the past. Not only is theology no longer the queen of the sciences, but it is facing the question whether it has any place at the university at all. Our experience today, namely that the theological faculties are being renamed as faculties for religious studies, is not really a new development. Surely, this is Harnack's nightmare come true. And while some of Harnack's arguments against these moves are obviously dated, or rather simply embarrassing, some might be timely and helpful today. One wonders, for example, whether Harnack's caveat of "unhealthy dilettantism" might indeed be the destiny of the religious departments as they try to do justice not only to Christian theology, but also other religions and movements. One needs to be careful here to avoid misunderstandings; hence, one could surely agree with David F. Ford who plans to "build departments and institutions that can be justified and nourished by more than one tradition."[55] This is beyond controversy, and our three theologians would undoubtedly agree. However, I would humbly argue that (Christian) theology still needs a "special place" at the university, to say it with Harnack. Theology must not cave in in face of today's threat of being sidelined. Theology deserves an independent faculty where scholars work in full academic freedom, for two reasons: first, because theology is a *Wissenschaft,* a science proper, and second, because theology is an essential member of the academy, as it facilitates communication both within the university and toward society and as it promotes unity. We shall briefly expand on these two issues in this concluding section.

Theology as Wissenschaft *Belongs to the University*

Harnack, Schlatter, and Kuyper in unison agree that theology is a proper academic subject that belongs to the university. In theology, we assess and make

54. Kuyper, *Lectures on Calvinism,* 139.

55. Ford, *The Future of Christian Theology* (Oxford: Wiley-Blackwell, 2011), 116.

propositional truth claims in similar ways as in other disciplines. As theologians we "create understanding" as Schlatter put it, as do members of the other faculties. The university's task is, according to Karl Jaspers, "to seek the truth as a community of scholars and students" *(die Wahrheit in der Gemeinschaft von Forschern und Schülern zu suchen).*[56] This certainly includes the theologian. Günther Thomas recently argued for theology's special role at the university as it represents a "truth-seeking community," whose own "subject's momentum" *(Eigendynamik des "Gegenstands")* makes it stand out in the "broad field of hermeneutical *Geisteswissenschaften.*"[57] Now the postmodern argument, of course, is that there is no objective truth out there, that knowledge is a social construct, always shifting and changing. The theologian who claims that she is actually seeking universal truth is labeled as a relic of a bygone (modern) era. If, however, according to this argument, theology is considered illegitimate, then one would also have to exclude the whole range of the humanities from the academic discourse. What, then, for example with philosophy? William Wood writes:

> [D]own the hall from the department of religion, we find another discipline, philosophy, with sterling academic credentials and its own methodological norms, norms that do seem to legitimate exactly the practice that our own opponents of theology will not countenance — namely, the practice of making and assessing truth claims about God.[58]

Surely, one would not want to show philosophy the door. Perhaps the postmodern argument, namely that no scientific discourse is able to claim universality, might actually work in theology's favor. For according to this argument one would have to consider theology in fact as justifiable as any other science. In other words, without universal norms one would have no basis on which one could exclude theology from the scientific community; theology would have to be considered as legitimate as any other academic subject.[59] This particular reading of postmodernism, then, in fact "provides an opportunity for

56. Jaspers, *Die Idee der Universität* (Berlin: Springer, 1946), 9.

57. Thomas, "Die Aufgabe der Evangelischen Theologie im Ensemble universitärer Religionsforschung: Eine Zumutung," 27.

58. Wood, "On the New Analytic Theology, or: The Road Less Traveled," *Journal of the American Academy of Religion* 77, no. 4 (2009): 958.

59. I am indebted to Dr. William Wood's line of argument as outlined in his paper, "Analytic Theology and the Academic Study of Religion," presented at the University of Edinburgh, School of Divinity, April 4, 2013.

the revitalization of *both* theology *and* religious studies," as Gavin Hyman concludes.[60]

Theology, then, is a proper *Wissenschaft*, or *wetenschap*, as Kuyper would have said. However, there will probably always remain what Kuyper called a "conflict of principles." If our theologians from the past encountered the modern atheistic presupposition, today one is confronted with postmodern pluralism, relativism, and secularism. Still, and here I am inclined to agree with Harnack et al., theology needs to take up this fight from the university — it is not to retreat to the "safer" theological seminary. Theology belongs to the university. For this is the place for the quest for truth. Here, we seek to discover and to spread truth by research and education, with integrity and precision, for the sake of the flourishing of human communities.

Theology Is Essential to the University

Second, theology is essential to the university as it promotes communication and unity. That is, theology is essential as it helps the other disciplines to fulfill what Schlatter called the university's religious-ethical task, which consists mainly in promoting communication both within the academy and between the academy and society. Theology as a proper member of the academy possesses unique links to other fields of research, such as linguistics, history, philosophy, anthropology, and sociology, and this makes theology an essential integrative element at the university, encouraging the members of the different disciplines to communicate with one another and to engage in lively discussion. Economists need good mathematicians, and so do physicists, medics, and biologists; yet one wonders whether they indeed converse with one another to an extent that allows for a fruitful collaboration. Unfortunately, theologians do not really exceed in setting a good example. One could certainly encourage cross-disciplinary conversation between the biblical studies scholar and the systematician, the church historian and the lecturer in apologetics. Theologians need to overcome their own internal boundaries and their isolationist mentality, rather promoting conversation, collaboration, and collegiality within the academy while also stimulating public debate in society as a whole.[61]

Theology never was and is never supposed to be a self-contained entity.

60. Hyman, "The Study of Religion and the Return of Theology," *Journal of the American Academy of Religion* 72, no. 1 (2004): 198.

61. See Ford, *The Future of Christian Theology*, 84-103.

The university, while being a "sovereign sphere," to use Kuyper's terminology, still influences the other spheres, such as society and the church. Theology, in particular, is, as Karl Barth reminds us, a "function of the church" *(eine Funktion der Kirche).* Our theology must thus not be confined to the ivory tower, but it is to offer its service to church and society. Our theology must be a public theology, as Abraham Kuyper reminds us, a public theology that is relevant today. Only as our theology becomes public, as it is applied to society and the church, does it justify its essential status at the university today.

Finally, theology is essential for the university as it promotes the "uni" in the *uni*-versity. When the university is in danger of developing into a "multiversity" or "di-versity," theology reminds the different disciplines of the big picture. That is, all fields of research are united as they attempt to understand God's revelation in his creation, in nature, and in history. In this regard, Harnack's Christological reminder, of Jesus Christ as the unifying center, is helpful. For as Christian theologians we believe that Jesus Christ is the *uni*versal savior, the "Savior of the world" (1 John 4:14). And the apostle Paul reminds us that "all things were created through him and for him. And he is before all things, and in him all things hold together" (Col. 1:16b-17). It is through Jesus Christ that our pursuit of knowledge finds its ultimate fulfillment — only through Jesus Christ will we know the truth, and the truth will set us free (John 8:32). Of course, the claim that a Jewish criminal, who was executed two thousand years ago, is still alive and is the Savior of the world still presents a stumbling block for (post)modern reason.[62] A conflict of principles will remain, and there will always be a tension in pursuing theology as an academic discipline at the university. Still, despite chronic frustration, we are called to embrace this tension. We are called to make a case for the *raison d'être* of our profession. In order to survive at the university, theology is to pursue its ethical task by focusing on what it can do best, namely by devoting itself to the canon of truth and by promoting conversation within the university context as well as with society as a whole, offering its service to the church and the public sphere, and thus serving toward the flourishing of human communities to the glory of God.

62. See 1 Corinthians 1:22-24.

Kuyper on the Teaching of History

Harry Van Dyke

No man was a greater believer in historical continuity than Abraham Kuyper. He conceived his life's calling to be to breathe new life into the Calvinism which surely was the cultural force that had made his small country great in the centuries between the Protestant Reformation and the French Revolution. At the same time he was convinced that Dutch Calvinism did not need to be *resurrected.* It wasn't dead: he had met it! He had met it among the common people in the parishes he had served. It was merely hidden, or half forgotten, or consigned by the enlightened progressives of his day to the "nachtschool" — the photophobic obscurantists in the land. Indeed, a disaster had descended upon the country during the Age of the Periwig, when Calvinism as a cultural force sank below the surface of national life. But that was the very reason why he, Kuyper, along with all the popular support he could muster, ought to try and raise it back to the surface and if possible help it retake the lead in the future development of the country. They hoped to do this, to be sure, while adjusting it so as to be "in rapport with the times," but always in continuity and solidarity with historic Calvinism.

This cultural campaign was to be waged under the banner of *Pro Rege.* After all, ever since Christ's ascension "the history of the nations of the world in its entirety is the theater of His kingly rule" (Kuyper 1912: 335). All people, all cultures, all ages are under one sovereign rule, whether they recognize it or not. Consequently, history is one, and mankind is one. Kuyper had learned to say with Edmund Burke[1] that the human race is united by an unbreakable

1. Kuyper's mentor, Groen van Prinsterer, had warmly recommended studying the "lead-

bond of those who now live, those who came before, and those who will come after: our race is a "beautiful work of art, conceived and created by God to his glory, intended to progress to ever richer attainments from generation to generation" (Kuyper 1905: 334).

On this view, education, particularly at home but also in the schoolroom, is critical for passing on the cultural achievements of the forefathers. Sound instruction in history is therefore indispensable, at two levels. The subject of *world* history commemorates the many things accomplished by man and the many wonders wrought by God. The subject of *national* history provides a means of vindicating a nation's uniqueness, hence of defending its independence. Keeping the history of one's country alive is crucial. "Great events, like a war of independence, do more to form and educate a people than the best school system" (Kuyper 1905: 385). Next to the Bible, history ranks among a nation's primary sources of inspiration. We all need national holidays, Kuyper writes, "to inspire our miserable present with the glory of the past" (Kuyper 1905: 450).

In his commentary on the antirevolutionary party's Program of Principles, Kuyper has a surprising take on the importance of teaching history aright. He does that in the context of outlining what makes for the strongest defense of a country: besides military means he draws attention to "moral means." And one of these moral means is the proper teaching of the history of the country. It is as if we hear Walter Scott or Thomas Carlyle when he writes:

> a wondrous mystery cleaves to that national history, a mystery that always attaches to an inspired and struggling life. It is a mystery that cannot be dissected in dates or exhausted in names and documents. Nor can it be unveiled by the most meticulous and pedantic description of what this or that historical figure thought and did and struggled through. It is a mystery that lies hidden *behind* those dates and names and individual exploits — in the nation's endurance during anxious times, in its sins during years of opulence, and in its gratitude to God in the hour of deliverance. The mystery of the collective life of a nation: it is invisible and ineffable. It redoubles the courage of the standard-bearer in the field of honor when he senses that

ing spokesmen of antirevolutionary politics," namely Edmund Burke, François Guizot, and Friedrich Julius Stahl. Kuyper, however, decided that he must also look into early Calvinist political thought, which for him included Hubert Languet, François Hotman, Philippe Du Plessis Mornay, and other publicists of the sixteenth century, as well as Oliver Cromwell and John Milton of the following century. See the correspondence between Groen and Kuyper in van Prinsterer 2002: 6:50, 66-69, 371, 414-15, 498.

the flag he clutches will decide the honor of a whole nation. It is elusive and indescribable. In moments of tension it stirs a slumbering people into righteous anger. . . .

Precisely the history of one's country harbors that *epic* quality that can inspire fresh deeds through remembering the past. It harbors that sense of unity which in moments of peril can take us out of our provincialism to face the foe arm in arm as one man. No less does it harbor those sublime signs indicating that the greatest things can often be accomplished with a very small force and that the most surprising results can be attained if against all hope one nevertheless ventures to rely on his God.

It is therefore essential for our people of all ranks and classes to be baptized once again with that holy enthusiasm for the history of our country. Not in memorizing tables and genealogies and reading dry chronicles, which never contained life to begin with and are therefore incapable of awakening life. Why not spare our simple folk all *that* baggage? It is a rare mother who knows how many ribs and how many vertebrae her child has; but she thinks, "The doctor will know that," and she just loves her child and shares its pranks over the fence with her neighbor. In the same way it makes no difference in the world to a child from the working classes if it is confused by a century or three and thinks that Orange lies in Frisia and William III was a son of Frederick Henry.[2] What matters for that child are the tableaus, the imaginary pictures in full color, the heroic figures, and even the legends of miraculous events. For without those legends your history, which is always a fallible narrative anyway, will no longer be real history; it will be without its truest, most inspiring element, that "mysterious breath of life."

Let the supporters of the Education Act [favoring the secular public schools] take heed. It is a fact that in the interest of their partisan intentions they have taken the soul out of our history, robbed it of warmth and life. Knowledge of our history has already dwindled considerably in the country. Under their system we will never again see a time when that history will have the power to inspire. They will have to answer to God and our people for allowing this breach in our moral defense for the sake of pushing their political agenda. (Kuyper 1880: §229)

2. The principality of Orange lies in southern France, and king-stadtholder William III (1650-1702) was a grandson of Prince Frederick Henry (1584-1647). An American equivalent would be to think that George Washington crossed the Delaware just south of Princeton in order to do battle with Confederate troops under Robert E. Lee, or that the boy who committed the vandalism of chopping down a cherry tree in his father's yard and owning up to it afterwards was honest Abe Lincoln.

Thus to take the soul out of Dutch history seriously weakens the nation. If the next generation is not taught what once constituted the inner strength and resilience of their people, the distortion of their history is but another strike against the public school. Kuyperians believed that the Christian school does not have religion as an add-on but as the yeast that is to leaven all instruction. "The three R's may be the same in all schools," Kuyper concedes, "but the Christian school is first of all different in the way it teaches history," and that is precisely how it contributes to "transmitting from generation to generation the Christian tradition, the Christian worldview and the Christian life-style" (Kuyper 1905: 391-92).

Accordingly, Kuyper argues unabashedly for a type of drums-and-trumpets history, the kind of history that "depicts the vitality of a nation, not the anatomy of a corpse" (Kuyper 1906: 35).

Can this praise of the teaching of history to the schoolchild possibly explain the fact that no historian was appointed at Kuyper's Free University until almost four decades into its existence?

A chronicler of a century of historical study in the Free University has offered a seemingly plausible explanation for this delay. If Kuyper has so little respect for facts, he writes, small wonder no historian was appointed: "Whoever treats history in this manner has no need for historical science. On the contrary, in fact. For scientific history will see it as its task to unmask the legends that Kuyper thinks constitute true history."[3]

Two pieces of evidence argue against this chronicler's explanation; one is rather obvious; the other requires a little searching.

My first piece of evidence is that Kuyper's praise of national history, as we just heard, refers to the teaching of history at the primary school level, not in an academic institution for higher learning. For this careless oversight our chronicler was roundly criticized shortly after his analysis appeared in print.[4] Is it likely that Kuyper would not have distinguished between the requirements of sound history instruction at the primary and at the tertiary level?

3. Van Deursen 1980: 360-400, at 368. It was unfortunate that the otherwise highly respected Van Deursen based his conclusion on the sociological deconstruction of Kuyper's "view of society" (Van Weringh 1967). That said, Van Deursen is correct (1980: 368-69) in critiquing the one-sidedness of Kuyperians in their rather selective use of history.

4. See W. Bakker in *Gereformeerd Weekblad,* 20 and 27 March and 3 and 10 April 1981. Equally careless is Van Deursen's dismissive comment (1980: 370) of the history lectures by Professor Fabius, who in addition to law also taught history in the first few years of the new university. In my estimation, the book by Paul Fabius dealing in the main with Hippolyte Taine's interpretation of the French Revolution — *De Fransche revolutie: eene studie* (Amsterdam, 1881) — is a serious piece of independent research.

The second piece of evidence relates to Kuyper's *actual search* for a suitable appointment to a chair in history at the newly founded Free University. It is found in a letter sent to Kuyper by one of his former teachers, the doyen of Dutch historians in the nineteenth century, Robert Fruin (1823-1899).[5] But before we look at the evidence I shall begin with where Fruin's letter begins:

> I have read your oration [*Souvereiniteit in eigen kring*] with great interest and am pleased to see that you, who once were my disciple,[6] have deservedly entered the ranks of the learned scholars. Not that I agree with you, which you do not expect anyway. In my opinion you have especially laid violent hands on history and appropriated a principle for your antirevolutionary system of which there was no question before the revolution. To name one example: who ever thought of the separation of church and state, of a free church in a free state, prior to the modern ideas that arose in America and England and were applied in France and elsewhere? In an odd sort of way you reverse the roles when you make out that state omnipotence is a modern concept and the concept of sovereignty (always limited, as you rightly emphasize) belongs to the anti-revolution. . . . Mill's excellent work *On Liberty* is well suited to convince you that the defenders of sphere-sovereignty, or better sphere-independence, are not all of *your* party.

After this brief lesson in liberal thought, Fruin continued by giving his friendly advice on a somewhat delicate subject. The subject was a possible first appointee to the history chair at the new Vrije Universiteit. Kuyper had been casting about and had sent a recent doctoral dissertation by one prospect to Professor Fruin for his opinion. The dissertation dealt with the relations and tensions between the *Réveil* and the *Afscheiding* — between the elitist evangelical Revival within the Dutch Reformed Church and the common man's Secession from that church in the first half of the nineteenth century.[7] Fruin's response was circumspect:

5. Fruin was a trailblazer in scientific history in the Rankean style. He wrote five full-length books and hundreds of shorter monographs, all dealing with aspects of modern Dutch history. His works were posthumously collected in 10 volumes by his pupils P. J. Blok, P. L. Muller, and S. Muller Fzn in *Verspreide Geschriften* (The Hague: Nijhoff, 1900-1905).

6. Kuyper had Fruin as his history teacher in Leiden's *gymnasium* and was able to follow his lectures in Leiden's Academy after Fruin's appointment in 1860 to the chair of Modern Dutch History.

7. Lútzen Harmens Wagenaar, *Het "Reveil" en de "Afscheiding"; bijdrage tot de Nederlandsche kerkgeschiedenis in de eerste helft der XIX eeuw* (diss. Utrecht; Heerenveen, 1880).

> I appreciate the thoroughness with which you are looking to fill the various chairs with the most suitable candidates and so I have read the dissertation you sent me with great care. . . . However, I have not been able to arrive at a definite conclusion. The study does the author credit and serves to recommend him. It is well organized, well formulated, and written with verve. But the subject itself, *deriving from the controversies of our day,* renders it unfit to serve as a touchstone. I honestly do not know what to advise.[8]

Fruin went on to suggest to Kuyper that if he *must* choose he should go by the impression the person makes on him, rather than by the merit of a single publication. For our purposes another part of Fruin's advice is of more immediate interest: he hesitates to recommend the man because he took his subject "from the controversies of our day."

Fancy that! For Kuyper, that would not at all have been a negative quality in a historian. On the contrary, it would have been a mark in his favor! If Fruin had meant to caution Kuyper against hiring the prospective candidate, he may well have nudged him toward hiring him. History for Kuyper could be a powerful tool to fight the culture war of his day, a veritable *"machine de guerre."* The liberals, with their enlightened but distorted view of the nation's history, were weaning the country away from its spiritual heritage, from the Calvinism that had once made the nation great. There was need of a historian who could wield his expertise as a weapon to set the record straight. Such a historian would fit right in with the whole purpose of the Free University. The movement headed by Kuyper, wrote a critic after his death, was less served by faithful descriptions of what really happened in the past, and much more by what one could do with it in the present.[9]

I referred just now to "the whole purpose of the Free University." That purpose was captured well in the dedication speech delivered in the prayer service on the eve of the university's opening, October 19, 1880. The text which Kuyper's associate, the Rev. Dr. Hoedemaaker, had chosen for his oration that evening was taken from 1 Samuel 13: "Now there was no smith found throughout all the land of Israel, for the Philistines said, Lest the Hebrews make swords or spears for themselves." Everybody knew who the "Hebrews" were in 1880, and who the "Philistines." The faithful in the land were systematically shut out from the culturally formative centers of the country; the few scholars among

8. Fruin to Kuyper, 7 Dec. 1880; in Smit and Wieringa 1957: 246-48 (emphasis added).

9. H. Colijn [F. C. Gerretson], "Levensbericht van Dr. A. Kuyper," in *Handelingen van de Maatschappij der Nederlandsche Letterkunde, 1922-1923* (Leyden: Brill, 1923), 41-63, at 53-54.

them were rarely appointed at the public universities, and careers in law and politics were all but closed to them. The Reformed people needed their own smithy, their own armory, to be a match for secular liberalism's onslaught on old-time religion and Calvinism's legacy as shapers of a prosperous and God-fearing country.[10]

The original dream — to establish a broadly based university for orthodox Protestantism — was noble but proved unattainable. Leaders of the broad confessional center in the national church, notably the "ethical-irenicals," backed off at critical moments. Perhaps they feared Kuyper's dominant — if not to say domineering — presence at the center of the proposed venture. And so, by default, the Free University became more or less a *neo-Calvinist* institution. The dreamed-of Free University could only be the initiative of the neo-Calvinists who would push it through against considerable odds and with a more narrowly defined constituency. It is a misreading of history to depict this development as proof of the deplorable narrow-mindedness or aggressive spirit of annexation on their part.[11]

Meanwhile, to ensure the neo-Calvinist character of the institution, it stated that it would base its instruction and research on "the Reformed principles." Vague though these principles were, the initiators appear to have assumed their collective agreement with them.[12] When fifteen years later a faculty committee tried to clarify what was meant by "the Reformed principles," their report to the university's Senate could only outline a roadmap that could *lead to* ascertaining their meaning (Kuyper 1895: 22). The eighteen theses in which this roadmap was laid out consisted of "a kind of

10. The message may seem somewhat at odds with Hoedemaaker's background. Philippus Jacobus Hoedemaaker (1839-1910), the son of Dutch immigrants, grew up in Kalamazoo, Michigan, where in secondary school he developed a lasting interest in the writings of Ralph Waldo Emerson. However, his upbringing at home was strictly Reformed, and after he returned to the country of his parents he became an accomplished theologian, specializing in exegesis and apologetics, particularly in his well-known book on Higher Criticism, *De Mozaïsche Oorsprong van de wetten in de boeken Exodus, Leviticus en Numeri* (Leiden, 1895; German trans., 1897). He would later oppose Kuyper's campaign for "a free church in a free state," claiming instead a permanent role for the one undivided Reformed Church in the government of the country and its entire population. Perhaps Emerson's holistic emphasis did have a lasting influence on Hoedemaaker's mind after all.

11. The rather complex story of the birth of the Free University is analyzed in Van Dijk 1979.

12. Only curator De Savornin Lohman demurred; he refused to have his conscience bound by them and instead claimed that it was enough to rely only on the guidance of Scripture. His position contributed to his dismissal as law professor in 1895.

intuitive plumbing"[13] of Calvinism's core beliefs at work in the history of Reformed churches and Calvinist nations, supplemented by (1) a brief reference to modern-day attention to the "knowing subject" as first analyzed by Immanuel Kant, and (2) a general guideline for the different disciplines, namely to always distinguish between "creation, fall and re-creation" in their objects of study.

In any event, this was the university that was in need of an appointment in History. And yet, in spite of the positive quality in the historian who had caught his notice, Kuyper, having received Fruin's thoughtful reply, does not appear to have urged Curators to appoint the man.[14] How to explain that he abandoned his original effort for an early appointment? Was he not sufficiently impressed by the personality of the man? Or could it be that for his fledgling academy he put greater store by a colleague of unquestioned and undisputed historical scholarship than by a fellow militant beside him in the trenches, constantly taking aim and opening fire on the enemy? After all, this was not a search for an inspiring schoolteacher, but for a qualified scholar. In any case, there would be no historian appointed at the Free University until almost four decades later.

The story of Kuyper's early effort to find a historian proves that our chronicler is again on shaky ground with his suggestion that Kuyper felt no need for such an appointment. There was a man available, but he had entered the lists with a controversial subject that was bound to stir up passions. And Kuyper may also have considered that the new and vulnerable university was probably best served for the time being by avoiding any negative publicity.

As for Kuyper himself, we should not forget that in the first phase of his career he combined his pastoral charge with intensive activities as a church historian. He was tireless in hunting down primary source materials throughout Europe's libraries and he was utterly exacting in the quality of publications to be sponsored by the organization he had founded for the history of the Reformation in the Netherlands, the Marnix Association, a consortium modeled somewhat after the Parker Society in Britain (Praamsma 1985: 65-72). His doctoral dissertation[15] was widely praised, and his critical edition of the

13. See Klapwijk 2013: 223.

14. Only a perusal of the minutes of Curators can provide certainty on this point. Since Van Deursen, who studied those minutes, makes no reference to any such nomination, we may safely assume that Kuyper never submitted one.

15. A. Kuyper, *Disquisitio historico-theologica, exhibens Johannis Calvini et Johannis à Lasco de ecclesia sententiarum inter se compositionem* (diss. Leyden; The Hague: Nyhoff, and Amsterdam: Muller, 1862).

complete works of the sixteenth-century Polish reformer Johannes à Lasco was a model of historical scholarship.[16]

Finally, there is still another possible reason why Kuyper might not necessarily have deemed the partisan religious credentials of a candidate of equal weight — let alone of greater weight — than his scholarly aptitudes. Many of Kuyper's principled positions had a practical side as well, since they were formulated upon close examination of everyday life. Take his emphasis on the *antithesis* in the world of higher learning: the gulf between the practice of scholarship by unregenerate worldlings and born-again Christians, between rival camps of academics engaged in relentless competition (Kuyper 1931: 130-39). For all that, Kuyper was sober-minded enough not to discount the reality of an area, however limited, of basic agreement and real consensus among scholars, thanks to God's preserving or common grace. That consensus, he holds forth, occurs not just in "material" disciplines like geology and physics but also in a "spiritual" science such as history:

> [I]n part at least, even the spiritual sciences deal with externally observable facts . . . such as in *History*, whose skeletal framework . . . consists entirely of events and facts that must be told on the basis of a wide variety of empirical evidence. . . . There is a broad area of research into details where one can earn his laurels without descending to the deepest contrasts between the two worldviews. . . . In this less demanding sort of research one can more quickly arrive at results that have greater certainty; many questions of a historical nature can be settled within this more limited horizon.

Kuyper is quite sure that nine out of ten scholars prefer to work at this more superficial level (Kuyper 1909: 106, 114). Perhaps he had concluded that his prospective candidate belonged more to these ninety percent.[17]

Obviously, Kuyper was pulled in several directions, but I believe that ultimately his vision for the teaching and writing of history, not just in the elementary classroom but equally in the lecture hall, is revealed in a comment he wrote when the greatest Dutch historian of his time had been laid to rest:

16. A. Kuyper, *Johannis à Lasco opera tam edita quam inedita,* 2 vols. (The Hague: Nyhoff, and Amsterdam: Muller, 1866).

17. Wagenaar by all reports was an affable man. In 1886 he sided with Kuyper's secession from the national church. He developed into an influential churchman and earned some fame as the author of popular biographies of great men in the history of the Reformation in the Netherlands; see J. C. Rullmann in *Christelijke Encyclopaedie* (1st ed.), 5:684-85.

> The very thing Robert Fruin lacked, and increasingly lost, was the enthusiasm that imparts an epic quality to the past. Precisely his meticulous research into the details of historical events rendered him increasingly immune to an *epic view* of the past. The microscope is not the instrument to make you marvel at the divinely exalted on the storm-tossed sea.[18]

REFERENCES

Fabius, Paul. 1881. *De Fransche revolutie: Eene studie.* Amsterdam.

Fruin, Robert. *Verspreide Geschriften,* ed. P. J. Blok, P. L. Muller, and S. Muller Fzn. The Hague: Nijhoff, 1900-1905.

Klapwijk, Jacob. 2013. "Abraham Kuyper on Science, Theology and University." In *On Abraham Kuyper: A Collection of Readings on the Life, Work and Legacy of Abraham Kuyper,* ed. Steve Bishop, 221-45. Sioux Center, IA: Dordt College Press.

Kuyper, Abraham. 1862. *Disquisitio historico-theologica, exhibens Johannis Calvini et Johannis à Lasco de ecclesia sententiarum inter se compositionem.* Diss. Leyden; The Hague: Nyhoff, and Amsterdam: Muller.

———. 1880. *"Ons Program."* Second, popular edition. Amsterdam: J. H. Kruyt.

———. 1895. *Publicatie van den Senaat der Vrije Universiteit, inzake het onderzoek ter bepaling van den weg die tot de kennis van de Gereformeerde beginselen leidt.* Amsterdam: J. H. Wormser.

———. 1905. *De Gemeene Gratie.* Vol. 3. Leiden: Donner, and Amsterdam: Höveker & Wormser.

———. 1906. *Bilderdijk in zijn nationale beteekenis.* Amsterdam and Pretoria: Höveker & Wormser.

———. 1909. *Encyclopaedie der Heilige Godgeleerdheid.* Vol. 2. Second, revised ed. Kampen: Kok.

———. 1912. *Pro Rege of het Koningschap van Christus.* Vol. 3. Kampen: Kok.

———. 1931. *Calvinism: Six Stone Lectures.* Grand Rapids: Eerdmans.

Praamsma, Louis. 1985. *Let Christ Be King: Reflections on the Life and Times of Abraham Kuyper.* Jordan Station, ON: Paideia Press.

Smit, H. J., and W. J. Wieringa, eds. 1957. *Correspondentie van Robert Fruin, 1845-1899.* Groningen: Wolters.

Van Dijk, A. J. 1979. "Wetenschap en Beginsel." *Beweging* 43: 28-36.

Van Deursen, A. Th. 1980. "De Vrije Universiteit en de geschiedwetenschappen." In *Wetenschap en Rekenschap, 1880-1980: Een eeuw wetenschapsbeoefening en wetenschapsbeschouwing aan de Vrije Universiteit,* ed. M. van Os and W. J. Wieringa. Kampen: Kok.

18. *De Standaard,* 29 June 1899; quoted in Van Weringh 1967: 59-60.

Van Prinsterer, G. Groen. 1920-1992. *Briefwisseling,* 6 vols. The Hague: Instituut voor Nederlandse Geschiedenis.
Van Weringh, Jac. 1967. *Het maatschappijbeeld van Abraham Kuyper.* Assen: Van Gorcum.

Abraham Kuyper and the Idea of a Christian Scholar

Gordon Graham

An academic journal entitled *The Christian Scholar* came into existence in 1953, and collapsed fifteen years later. Its creation was one manifestation of a sudden, new-found confidence in the idea that Christian theology, in the broadest sense, was highly relevant to the world of scholarship, and could provide one answer to a critical situation that had arisen as a result of the rapid expansion of colleges and universities in North America. The crisis did not have to do with financial resources. The rise in student numbers had greatly strengthened these, as had hugely increased federal funds for research. Rather, the crisis was perceived to be an intellectual one, to do with the nature of the university itself — what was its unifying purpose? Did it have any? A multiplication, and fragmentation, of subjects and disciplines had accompanied this expansion in higher education, so that between the natural sciences, the social sciences, the humanities and professional studies, there now seemed to be little connection. The common aim that degree awarding institutions had previously been thought to share had disintegrated. The ever-increasing emphasis on socially useful scientific and technological research seemed to relate very poorly, if at all, to the old ideal of a liberal education for an educated citizenry.

I

The Christian Scholar was created with the hope of speaking to this identity crisis. By locating academic inquiry within a single theological vision it would thereby demonstrate the continuing, indeed indispensable, relevance of Christianity to the rationale of the university, and thus to the intellectual underpinnings of society as a whole. The journal subsequently collapsed, and though a different journal — *The Christian Scholar's Review* — took its place, it had a much more restricted ambition. The intellectually formative role envisaged for *The Christian Scholar* never really materialized. Partly, this was because of factors beyond anyone's control. Such rapidly changing circumstances worked powerfully against the possibility of *any* single, unifying vision. In particular, the expansion brought huge numbers of new academics into the system, many from social and educational backgrounds that had little or no previous connection with the academic world, and to whom, consequently, the older ideal of the university meant nothing. Moreover, the members of this new generation of faculty were mostly launched on career trajectories that gave pride of place to personal academic advancement, a "publish or perish" culture reinforced by the requirements and expectations of professional guilds. The probability that a single institutional goal could command widespread attention, still less general consensus, was almost zero, regardless of how intellectually cogent the articulation of that goal might be. The conditions that underlay the "crisis," ironically, were the very same conditions that made the most coherent solutions to it impossible.

But more strikingly for present purposes, the problem was not simply that a single voice could no longer expect to be heard across the sector. The voices claiming to be Christian were not united; they gave uncertain and often conflicting messages. What was Christianity's distinctive conception of the nature and value of scholarship? Key to answering this was a further crucial question. Was the "knowledge" of God that Christians claimed to find in the Bible, and in religious experience, genuine knowledge, which is to say, epistemologically equivalent to the knowledge that modern universities were so successfully producing by means of experiments, quantitative methods, and empirical evidence? If so, by what criterion could this equivalence be demonstrated? Confronted by this question, Christian scholars, it seemed, had no straightforward answer to which they all subscribed.

The question whether Christian scholarship can be at one and the same time both distinctively Christian and *bona fide* intellectual inquiry remains largely unanswered. It is common for the "mission statements" of church-related colleges and universities to declare a double obligation — a commitment to "academic excellence" on the one hand and to "Christian values" on the other. But it is very rare for the relation between the two to be set out with any precision. In reality, it is often evident that the two goals are institutionally confined to quite separate spheres. Thus Christian "values" are promoted in chapel worship, social outreach, and pastoral counseling, while in lecture halls and laboratories "academic excellence" is left to rule supreme. Though the Christian religion may still be promoted as in some sense "true," it turns out to be a different kind of "truth" to that which scientific and historical inquiry is expected to uncover, even in Christian colleges.

This bifurcation may work reasonably well in some contexts. Applied to the case of education and research in the theological subjects themselves, however, it seems especially problematic. Is theology an academic inquiry like any other, and if so, do its results stand four square with the results of other inquiries? Can theology tell us about God, or only about "beliefs about" God? For several decades now there has been an evident reluctance to answer this question with a confident and resounding "yes."

Theology, of course, has always been located within professional schools, and this rightly sustains the inclination to focus on theological *education,* which is to say, provision of the knowledge and the practical skills likely to prove useful to pastors and ministers. Such a conception is essentially technical, however, and while from this point of view theological educators can be regarded as producers, and not merely transmitters, of useful knowledge, the ways in which theological inquiry might be valuable within the world of scholarship, and in its own right, is left unexplained. So much so, in fact, that not infrequently it is passed over in silence.

There is a telling example of this silence close to home. In 2012 the Trustees of Princeton Theological Seminary endorsed a Strategic Plan by which to guide the institution as it heads into its third century. The Plan is one that seeks to serve the Church by re-orienting the seminary to new national and international contexts. Against this background, institutional "imperatives" are set out that aim to ensure the training of clergy better equipped for the Church in contemporary America, and better stewardship of educational resources for the benefit of the global Church as a whole. Nowhere in this lengthy document, however, is scholarship expressly mentioned, or its role explicitly considered. Consequently, the purpose of scholarly research and publication on the part of Faculty, for which generous provision continues to be made, is left obscure. Christian teachers labor for the sake of their students. For whose benefit do Christian *scholars* labor? Is it the academy? Or is it the Church? "It is *both*," many people would like to be able to answer, but this simply raises a further question: How can a single activity serve two ends that now seem so significantly different?

I do not suppose that Princeton Seminary's Strategic Plan is unique in its failure to clarify the role of scholarship in its activities. On the contrary, I am inclined to think that the absence of clarity on this issue is a mark of our times. If so, the contrast with the Netherlands in the late nineteenth century could hardly be sharper. For in *that* context, Abraham Kuyper saw not merely the possibility, but the *necessity,* and hence the desirability, of a modern university founded *entirely* upon Christian principles. And with his usual, astonishing energy, he set about creating it in the form of Amsterdam's Free University. Kuyper's creation still exists and holds a respected place among European universities. Whether, and to what extent, it continues to realize his vision for it, is not a topic upon which I am competent to comment, and in any case not one for the present occasion. The question here is whether there is any element in the thinking that lay behind it that might illuminate our contemporary condition.

It must be acknowledged, of course, that that was then, and this is now. Perhaps the world has changed in ways that would thwart even a level of energy and commitment as great as Kuyper's. In this paper I shall not argue to the contrary. My aim is the much more modest one of exploring some of the issues surrounding the very idea of Christian scholarship. But I hope to show that some of Kuyper's thoughts can still be made to throw light on them.

II

The central issue confronting people who call themselves Christian scholars is the problem of integrity. This problem is usually conceived in quasi-moral terms. Scholarly integrity requires us to follow the argument wherever it leads and to endorse only those conclusions that square with the evidence. Scholarship brings with it a primary commitment to truth, and this means that no conclusion can properly be excluded from the outset. Christian integrity, on the other hand, rests on faithfulness to the Bible as revelation and the witness of the Church, even in the face of major intellectual objections. It appears, then, that Christian scholars face the perpetual threat of divided loyalties. People can be both scholars and Christians, certainly, and they may never actually find themselves torn between the two. But their position is one in which there remains the ever present possibility that intellectual inquiry degenerates into apologetics.

A recurrent response to this view of the matter has sought a solution by invoking a dualism of some kind. One familiar version contrasts "faith" with "knowledge," making Christian discipleship a matter of faith, and knowledge the aim of scholarly activity. Interpreted in one way, however, this dualism does not *solve* the problem; it simply denies its existence. If "faith" is thought of primarily in conative or affective rather than cognitive terms — as an existential choice, or an emotional disposition — then it is indeed true that "faith" does not have cognitive goals that could conflict with the "knowledge" the scholar seeks. But the further implication of this is that scholarship does not fall within the province of "faith" at all, because faith is not an exercise of the intellect. To "resolve" the conflict between Christian faith and intellectual inquiry in this way, accordingly, seems a rather hollow triumph.

There is, however, a different and more promising way in which this duality may be interpreted, one that attributes to both sides properly cognitive goals that are nevertheless importantly distinct. This alternative interpretation is often employed in attempts to resolve the perceived conflict between "religion" and "science" — and using the terminology of Stephen J. Gould — declares religion and science to be different *magisteria,* each with its own criteria of validity. The duality invoked here can be extended significantly, to demarcate not merely religion from science, but all "the humanities" from all "the sciences," social as well as natural. This is a dualism that has commanded quite wide support within the academy as an important corrective to contemporary fashion. The indisputable success of the natural sciences has given the modern world something of an obsession with knowledge as the goal of intellectual inquiry, and pressured most other subjects into modeling their rather different forms of inquiry in terms that are seriously distorting to any conception of liberal learning. The distortion arises from a failure to distinguish "truth" from "meaning," and knowledge from understanding, and hence to ignore the fact that meaning and understanding are equally important cognitive values. Indeed, the formulation and critical scrutiny of frameworks of understanding is essential to anything properly called inquiry, since without it the successful acquisition of new "knowledge" cannot have any cognitive significance.

There is something importantly right about this dualism, it seems to me, because it is easy to cite instances of genuine knowledge that are entirely lacking in any value or significance. The number of blades of grass beneath my foot as I stand on my lawn would be an example. There is a truth of the matter about this, but it is not a truth that anyone has any reason to seek or to value. So *real* knowledge can be *trivial,* which shows that the set of cognitive values must be wider than knowledge of the truth, and indeed that truth needs this wider context if it is to have any intellectual significance.

Still, the duality of knowledge and meaning has to be explicated carefully. That is because it is so easily conflated with two other dualisms, the power of whose destructive influence on modern thought would be hard to exaggerate.

One is the supposition of a radical division between "fact" and "value." The other is a sharp contrast between "objective truth" and "subjective opinion." If these three distinctions are run together, as they often are, then "meaning" quickly becomes a matter of subjectively endorsed values, while "knowledge" alone commands the validating sanction of objectively determined truth. Construed in this way, scholarly inquiry is confined to uncovering, articulating, and elaborating the various systems of meaning that have arisen and found favor in the history of the world. It cannot give cognitive endorsement to some systems over others. It cannot accord higher status to systems of meaning that are cognitively rich in comparison with others that have been generated in entirely affective ways, or simply been bequeathed by cultural tradition.

In the case of "religion," the dominance of this way of thinking is almost complete. The religions of the world, it is widely held, are to be interpreted as "systems of meaning" multiply realized in social practices, cultural artefacts, and literary works. The existence of such systems opens up endless possibilities for scholarly work — recording, preserving, describing, interpreting. But the scholar *qua* scholar does not pass judgment on the meaningfulness of a system of meaning. It is what it is. Christians can be anthropologists, historians, literary scholars, musicologists, or art historians, and some of their contributions to scholarship may, as it happens, provide fellow Christians with illuminating materials for their own pursuit of faith. Nevertheless, viewed in this light, the connection between their own religious adherence and their scholarly activities is a purely contingent one. Their faith and work are no more conceptually connected than in the case of someone who is, say, both a Christian and a heating engineer.

III

If this contingent dualism is the best we can do, we must conclude, I think, that the *idea* of a Christian scholar is incoherent. In times past, when "Christendom" was to be characterized as a near universal and largely unquestioned "system of meaning," the position may have been different. In what has come to be known, and widely acknowledged, as a "multicultural" world, Christian scholarship can at most amount to the scholarly exploration of what happens to be our own tradition. This exploration may uncover some new facts and insights that will be of interest to the academy in general, insofar as others — Christian and non-Christian — are engaged in a similar exploration. And perhaps such scholarly insights are more likely to come from those who have a special sympathy with their subject matter. To this extent, then, even if the relation is a contingent one, scholars who are also avowedly Christian can have a valuable contribution to make to their subject areas.

It was to something like this rather lame role that Abraham Kuyper was responding when he pressed for the establishment of a Christian university, and rejected the suggestion that Christian scholarship might be equally well served by the appointment of a few explicitly "Christian" chairs in an otherwise secular university. From such an arrangement, Kuyper says,

> Everyone would get the impression that real science proceeds from the unbelieving world, that there it receives its power and urge, that there its temple is built, and that the Christian religion has no higher calling than to exercise some criticism here and there and, if possible, to offer a little correction. The tree would still be bad, still grow from a cankered root, and all we would do on our part is cut off some useless branches, weed out some nettles, and here and there drape the branches with some plucked flowers that are destined to wither away before people notice them.[1]

To settle for this arrangement, he says, would be "to satisfy ourselves with the role of sauntering around another garden, clipper in hand." In asserting his alternative to this unsatisfactory position, Kuyper continues the biological metaphor. Scholarship must be rooted in something. Otherwise it is idle. But what it is rooted in makes all the difference to the direction in which it proceeds. To suppose that inquiry can be "free" in the sense of being independent of all presuppositions and orientations is a twofold error. In the first place, it divorces the acquisition of knowledge from the sort of grounding which alone makes knowledge possible, and in the second place it necessarily misconstrues the intellectual formation of human beings. The two points are connected.

> [A]ll knowledge proceeds from faith of whatever kind. You lean on God, you proceed from your own ego, or you hold fast to your ideal. . . . How could someone whose thinking lacked a starting point ever investigate something scientifically? . . . Any organic thinker rightly scoffs at the atomistic pretension that everyone, growing up, must think through all systems, search through every confession, and then choose the one he considers the best. No one can do this, and no one does. Neither the time nor the mental energy is available. Only some naïf, who does not yet understand higher

1. James D. Bratt, ed., *Abraham Kuyper: A Centennial Reader* (Grand Rapids: Eerdmans, 1998), 479. Hereafter, page references from this reader are given parenthetically in the text.

> learning, can fancy that he or someone else has accomplished this. Such sampling of all systems merely fosters superficiality. (486)

What Kuyper here refers to as "faith" might less misleadingly be called "reliance" since faith is often taken to mean doctrinal subscription. It is not true that in order to engage in systematic investigation (science) everyone needs some set of foundational beliefs that together make up a personal "credo" of some sort. What is true, however, is that all inquirers necessarily rely on some method or means of inquiry. This reliance cannot itself be validated without opening up an infinite regress. As critics of Descartes have long pointed out, the pursuit of an infallible method of inquiry, while easily construed as a requirement of rationality, is in fact impossible. Descartes did not actually empty his mind of all accumulated presuppositions in favor of "clear and distinct ideas." He could not do so, and only succeeded in throwing doubt on the deliverances of sense experience by implicitly relying on the *a priori* reasoning that generated those doubts. The natural scientist, similarly, relies upon methods that science, necessarily, cannot itself validate. To think otherwise is to suppose that scientific *method* could be subjected to scientific *scrutiny*. But what procedures is this scrutiny to follow, except the very procedures that are supposed to be under investigation? Furthermore, scientists neither choose nor invent these methods for themselves. They are inducted into the practice of science, and the point of such induction is not methodological innovation, but the mastery of established methods that come inextricably entwined with a stock of questions and problems that their use is intended to solve.

The implications of this important line of thought, however, are frequently misconstrued. From the fact that all rational inquiry must rely upon a method that it cannot validate, it does not follow that all methods are equally good. It only follows that no method can ever be uniquely good by avoiding this reliance. Clearly, there can be better and worse methods of inquiry just as there can be better and worse ways of securing any goal. Astronomy rightly displaced astrology, and chemistry alchemy. These examples are especially good illustrations of the fact that the methods of the natural sciences, which rely on observation, experiment, abstraction, and quantification, are superior to the methods of the pseudo-sciences that preceded them. These methods are held in high esteem, precisely because the success with which they have been used is indisputable.

There is however, this further issue. Even the most successful methods may be limited in their application. Observation, experiment, abstraction, and quantification have been hugely productive of new knowledge, knowledge about the worlds revealed to us in physics, chemistry, and biology. But can they be made to encompass all that we want to inquire into? Here we return to the distinction between truth and meaning, knowledge and understanding.

Kuyper addresses precisely this issue in the section of *Common Grace* recently published in English under the title *Wonder and Wisdom*. In it he draws a distinction between "lower" and "higher" science. Truth is the province of lower science, which consists in careful observation and the collection of facts. Higher science reaches beyond truth. "From making many observations higher science proceeds to compose a complex theory that clearly explains relevant causes, operative principles, and interconnectedness of phenomena. . . . [I]ndependent observations provide the material for higher science, although they do not yet constitute that science itself" (65).

Kuyper then goes on to note that over the course of the century in which he was writing, this important distinction had become increasingly ignored, so that people became "accustomed to supposing that such artificial observation already constituted the actual science, and from this premise they ascribed the highest scientific character to the observation of nature." They thus bestowed upon "lower" science a status it did not warrant and could not sustain. The effect, however, was to weaken the epistemological credentials of all those "sciences" in which observation played little or no part. "In this position," he says, "lurk an error and a danger" (65). The error was a false emphasis on truth; the danger was a misconstruction of the human mind that required everything properly called science to be materialistic. *Of course* every inquirer seeks truth, Kuyper says. The main question, though, is what truth is sought *for*. Truth in itself does not constitute wisdom or understanding, and however firmly grounded in observation, it still awaits explanation. Explanations, of course, compete, and even the best minds may dispute and disagree, or hold our best explanations to be, at most, provisional. The attraction of "truth" based on observation as an epistemological ideal is that it seems to guarantee convergence. If something is true, and known to be true, who can dispute it? The sleight of hand that follows, concludes from this that (as Kuyper expresses it) "only that is scientific which can be proven to the consent of all." Kuyper regards this claim as "absurd," and so indeed it is. If universal consent were the necessary condition of a proposition's being truly scientific, there could be no revision, correction, or amendment, in short, no science at all. Even more importantly, such an "ideal" of pure observation signals a return to "the old concept that our mind is a *tabula rasa*, a blank sheet of paper," without any content of its own — a simple recording device, an "elegant photographic camera" (66). Applied to physics and chemistry, Kuyper says, the damage done by this way of thinking is limited. But when it is carried over to "history, philosophy or any other human science" the effect is disastrous — an "increasing materializing of all science, feeding the false notion that all spiritual life arose from material causes" and the elimination of the independent spiritual life that makes the mind what it is.

The conclusion we should draw is that the incontestable successes of the observational sciences have led to a highly inflated estimation of their epistemological status. There is no denying that careful observation, abstraction, and quantification have proved to be valuable methods in some very successful natural sciences. The error is to suppose, on the strength of this fact, that the same methods should, or even could, be employed by all forms of human inquiry. To suppose otherwise is to imagine that reading a text requires nothing more than a clear view of the page.

IV

So far so good. Kuyper's observations on these matters, even if they are not now novel, are nonetheless well worth repeating, because the prejudice in favor of quantification and empirical observation as the true marks of "science" remains a very strong one. Moreover, breaking the hold that this idea has on contemporary ways of thinking must begin by exposing the unwarranted conflation of "impartiality" with neutrality and passivity, and undermining the false construction put upon the distinction between subjectivity and objectivity. Still, it is not entirely obvious what all this has to do with the idea of Christian scholarship, or the problems with which we began. How do Kuyper's reflections help us to avoid the degeneration of scholarship into apologetics, or explain the ways in which Christian scholarship can serve both academy and church?

We can start to make a little headway with these issues by rehearsing some of Kuyper's conclusions. First, scholarly inquiry is committed to truth, objectivity, and impartiality, but the mere fact that a scholar has a Christian allegiance does not in itself show that these are in any way threatened. *All* inquiry presupposes *some* allegiance to methods and concepts that scholars have not fashioned for themselves. So it would need to be shown that Christian allegiance carries some special danger. Dogmatism is just such a danger, of course, but it is not an intellectual fault confined to Christians. Second, scholarly inquiry neither seeks, nor can it plausibly offer, universal consensus. The very best inquiries into any matter of any complexity inevitably prompt dissent and disagreement. These are, indeed, the drivers of academic life. It is *doubts* about the findings of other scholars that stimulate further inquiry. So the fact that a Christian view of some matter will not command universal assent does not tell against its scholarly relevance or cogency. Third, the methods of the "exact" sciences are necessarily limited in their application. Not everything that exists can be observed, and not everything that can be observed can be measured or quantified. To insist that the unobservable is necessarily a function or product of the observable is the expression of a groundless metaphysical dogma, and ironically in conflict with itself, since we never observe the animate emerging from the inanimate.

All this, let us agree, is correct. Even so, the nature of Christian scholarship (as opposed to scholarship conducted by Christians) has yet to be made evident. On this matter, though, Kuyper himself is very clear. "Unbelieving science and the science done by believing Christians are two." Consequently, "what we need is a whole edifice of science built on a Christian foundation" (101), and this explains, of course, the foundation of the Free University. Why are they two? Science (and scholarship) investigate different kinds of phenomena — the natural and the spiritual. Everyone is in accord about this, but while atheistical science supposes that spirit is to be explained in terms of nature, Christian science supposes the reverse — that the natural world is to be explained as an emanation of spirit, ultimately of God who is pure spirit.

This difference necessitates alternative methodologies. Atheistical science seeks explanatory theories based upon facts that are established by empirical methods. Christian science, by contrast, requires revealed as well as established truths. To this extent Kuyper agrees with Kant; the methods of natural reason cannot themselves disclose the animating purposes of God. For this we need divine revelation, and to deny the existence of revelation is to forgo properly spiritual explanations. Christian science, then, leaves space for revealed truth, and it lends rational authority to the Scriptures as one important depository of it. "Unbelieving" science relies solely on the faculties of the human mind, and treats the Scriptures like any other collection of ancient documents.

The lessons Kuyper draws from this are not especially helpful in answering the questions with which we began. Christian scholarship, by his account, has no role in the modern academy because it must assert itself in opposition to the scholarship of the secular world. Insofar as it relates to it at all, it is in an apologetical role. "It is our duty," he says, "to take hold of scholarship as an instrument for propagating our convictions" (475). In short, the dualism to which Kuyper ultimately appeals is so deep that it implies some sort of academic apartheid. Believing and unbelieving science are as oil and water. The most we can expect by way of conversation is rhetorical exchange across the boundaries. This is not a conclusion that it is easy to accept now. For good or ill, most Christian scholars and scientists must secure their intellectual credentials in an academy that is not itself Christian. To withdraw to a separate enclave is not an option, and in any case would effectively concede that as Christians they have *nothing* to offer the secular academy.

The proper answer, as it seems to me, is to go with Kuyper only part of the way. The presuppositions of quantitative empirical science limit its applicability. Despite the aspirations of some varieties of political science, economics, psychology, sociology, and the like, the study of the human mind and the social world must proceed quite differently. But in a similar fashion, the appeal to revelation is also limited in its applicability. For the most part, I shall assert, the investigations of the "exact sciences" — physics, chemistry, biology, astronomy, mathematics, and so on — have no need of revealed truth, and to treat the book of Genesis, for instance, as relevant to them brings all the dangers with which we are familiar. The story of "Intelligent Design" is not an edifying one. On the other hand, to suppose that history, politics, ethics, social theory, anthropology, and so on can proceed in every instance without elements of the guiding framework inherited from Christianity seems equally wrong. They can of course appear to do so, and indeed, they can get quite far. But as Herman Bavinck pointed out illuminatingly in the case of the historical sciences, there are depths of understanding that positivism of this kind cannot plumb.

> If history is to be truly history, if it is to realize values, universally valid values, we cannot know this from the facts in themselves, but we borrow this conviction from philosophy, from our view of life and of the world — that is to say, from our faith. . . . The more we penetrate in our thinking to the essence of history, as to that of nature, the more it will manifest itself as rooted in revelation and as upborne by revelation.[2]

Conceived in this way, Christian scholarship does not seek to displace or counter secular science, but to pursue more promising avenues of inquiry — as and where these exist. To do so effectively, of course, it must be both honest and confident about its epistemological suppositions. The crucial point, though, is to affirm that they are indeed *epistemological,* which is to say, not merely declarations of "faith" that serve as badges of identity, but genuine aids to inquiry. The origins of language, the nature and function of emotion,

2. Herman Bavinck, *Philosophy of Revelation* (Grand Rapids: Eerdmans, 1953), p. 135.

the concept of political authority are all topics that naturalistic science has great difficulty in explaining properly. This is because, in Bavinck's words, the "universally valid values" that make language, emotion, and authority the things that they are, cannot be derived from "the facts in themselves." Christian scholarship is both Christian and scholarly when it is motivated by the desire for better explanations of phenomena such as these, and when it invokes distinctively Christian elements solely for this purpose. *Pace* Kuyper, it loses credibility in the academy by using scholarship as an instrument for propagating Christian convictions, and will re-establish its academic credentials when it uses Christian convictions to bring new illumination to the acknowledged problems of scholarship.